THE WORD ON INTENTION

"Dan and Amy are two of the most creative people I know. While creativity is not an innate talent, you can truly tell that this skill is something they nurture, expand, and grow daily. What they do well is unlock the secrets of multiple avenues leading to critical creativity through the nuances of understanding curricular content. Because they believe creativity works best with parameters and prompts, they have concocted a series of truly dazzling dishes that will definitely delight a diverse set of learners. I truly appreciate that Dan and Amy didn't just stop there but sought to add additional extension ideas for each lesson that add depth through multiple curricular pathways and additional applications."

—**Lisa Johnson** (@TechChef4u), author of *Cultivating Communication in the Classroom*

"*Intention* challenges the status quo and nudges the realities of our current learning structures in a significant way. The book makes it clear that creativity is the catalyst that we need for a deep sense of learning, a more meaningful dialogue, and a fresh joy in our classrooms."

—**Dr. Robert Dillon**, director of innovative learning, School District of University City

"Jam packed full of imaginative ideas for teachers. If you're struggling to inject a little creativity into your classroom, this book will give you all the inspiration you need."

—**Steve Wheeler**, teacher educator, Plymouth Institute of Education, U.K.

"This isn't a book about how to make art, it's a book about how to think.

"How many times I've said to my students, 'Be creative!' but didn't give them the tools do so? *Intention* is a toolbox for creative problem-solving in the classroom—a set of skills none of us can live without."

—**Michael Hernandez**, media arts teacher and consultant

"*Intention* will fill the gap for educators who want to bring critical creativity, meaningful making, and purposeful play into the classroom. I can't wait to see how educators hack the different catalogs to give all students the opportunity to share what they've learned through creative means."

—**Colleen Graves**, maker teacher librarian

"Burvall and Ryder have put together both inspiring motivation for teachers to take chances in their classrooms and actionable strategies that will work across grade levels and content areas. Since they are full time educators themselves, Burvall and Ryder's book reads like the combination of an honest memoir and a how-to pathway to creative energy-filled classrooms."

—**Kerry Gallagher**, JD, digital learning specialist at St. John's Prep in Danvers, Massachusetts, director of K–12 Education at ConnectSafely.org, EdSurge columnist

"This is a book that EVERY teacher must read. It is a book, not about art, but the way of the artist. In and ever-changing world, it must be packed into your valise to enable each of us to find our way. As such, this is a book for every one of us—parents, leaders, creatives.... Amy and Dan dance with us along a pathway of creative context and principles in a carefully choreographed journey that blends ideas and practise, allowing the reader to enjoy their dreaming and provoke new ideas."

—**Dave Strudwick**, headteacher, Plymouth School of Creative Arts, U.K.

"At first pass you can tell there is much to this book, but once immersed within Amy and Dan's world you find it keeps unfolding. The catalog of activities is not just another collection of assignments. With their suggestions for application and amplification, each is a launch point for any teacher to transform the depth and breadth of their teaching with creativity and media. You get not only the energy and creativity of these #ChampionsOfWhimsy but you are also getting the wisdom of two experienced classroom teachers who have been putting these ideas into action for a long time. And the stealth gain is that as you begin to teach with the approaches of ***Intention***, as you engage in rigorous whimsy, you will open up your creative powers too."

—**Alan Levine**, cogdogblog.com

"Few books make you smile. This is one of them. This book has so many ideas and exercises it would be impossible to read, use and absorb it without feeling more creative and more inspired to stimulate creativity in others. The book is rammed full of ideas spilling out from the pages."

—**Nigel Paine**, author, broadcaster coach in leadership learning and technology @ebase

"Burvall and Ryder distill the essence of what it means to be a creator, giving us all permission to unleash creativity in our classrooms with beautiful recipes of creative constraints. Their collaboration is certain to spark a new wave of creative intention in classrooms everywhere. ***Intention*** is more than a must-read, it is a must do! No matter your content area, this book is inspired, and it's for you. #morewhimsy #moreintention #lessexcuses #lessstandard"

—**Kelly Tenkely**, founder and CEO of Anastasis Academy and The Learning Genome Project

"In an ever-changing global landscape, one of increased connectivity and technological innovations like never before, creativity is at the forefront of reshaping the way classrooms operate and educators do their jobs. ***Intention*** takes the nuanced and often misdefined twenty-first-century learning skill of creativity and makes it an accessible and achievable learning objective in the classroom. Follow Amy and Dan's advice. Your learners will thank you."

—**Trevor Mackenzie**, educator and author of ***Dive Into Inquiry***

"***Intention*** offers you an opportunity to participate in an experience, and to deeply engage with what Burvall and Ryder refer to as 'critical creativity.' This is a DIY, 'how to guide,' that you can remix and mashup, curate, and critique. You'll discover tools and tactics that represent practical, pedagogical approaches to teaching and learning. With theoretical underpinnings that honour creativity as birthright, the ideas in this book support the development of a rich education, built on the foundations of cognitive agility and flexibility.

"If, as McLuhan says, 'the medium is the message,' through these pages you can become part of this important dialogue."

—**Cathy Hunt** (@art_cathyhunt), arts educator, advocate, advisor, author, and founder of iPadartroom.com

intention

critical creativity in the classroom

Amy Burvall and Dan Ryder

Intention

These books are available at special discounts when purchased in quantity for use as premiums, promotions, fundraising, and educational use. For inquiries and details, contact the publisher: edtechteam.com/press.

Editing and production by My Writers' Connection
Cover Design by Genesis Kohler
Infographic-styled author photos courtesy of Meg Willing
Iconography designed by Taylor Kaminsky
Credit to Blake Dain for vectorizing of Amy's sketches
Skateboarder image on page 132 courtesy of Sean Ziebarth

Published by EdTechTeam Press
Library of Congress Control Number: 2017941989
Paperback ISBN: 978-1-945167-32-4
eBook ISBN: 978-1-945167-33-1

Irvine, CA

For Gwenivere Ida—the girl with the answers to the questions they never ask. May you live, learn, and love like an artist all your days.

—Amy Burvall

For Avery and Maddox, who make each new day better than the last with their unconditional love, hugs, and LEGO.

For my own Amy, without whom nothing I have, and nothing that I am, would be.

—Dan Ryder

WHAT'S
INSIDE

AMY BURVALL

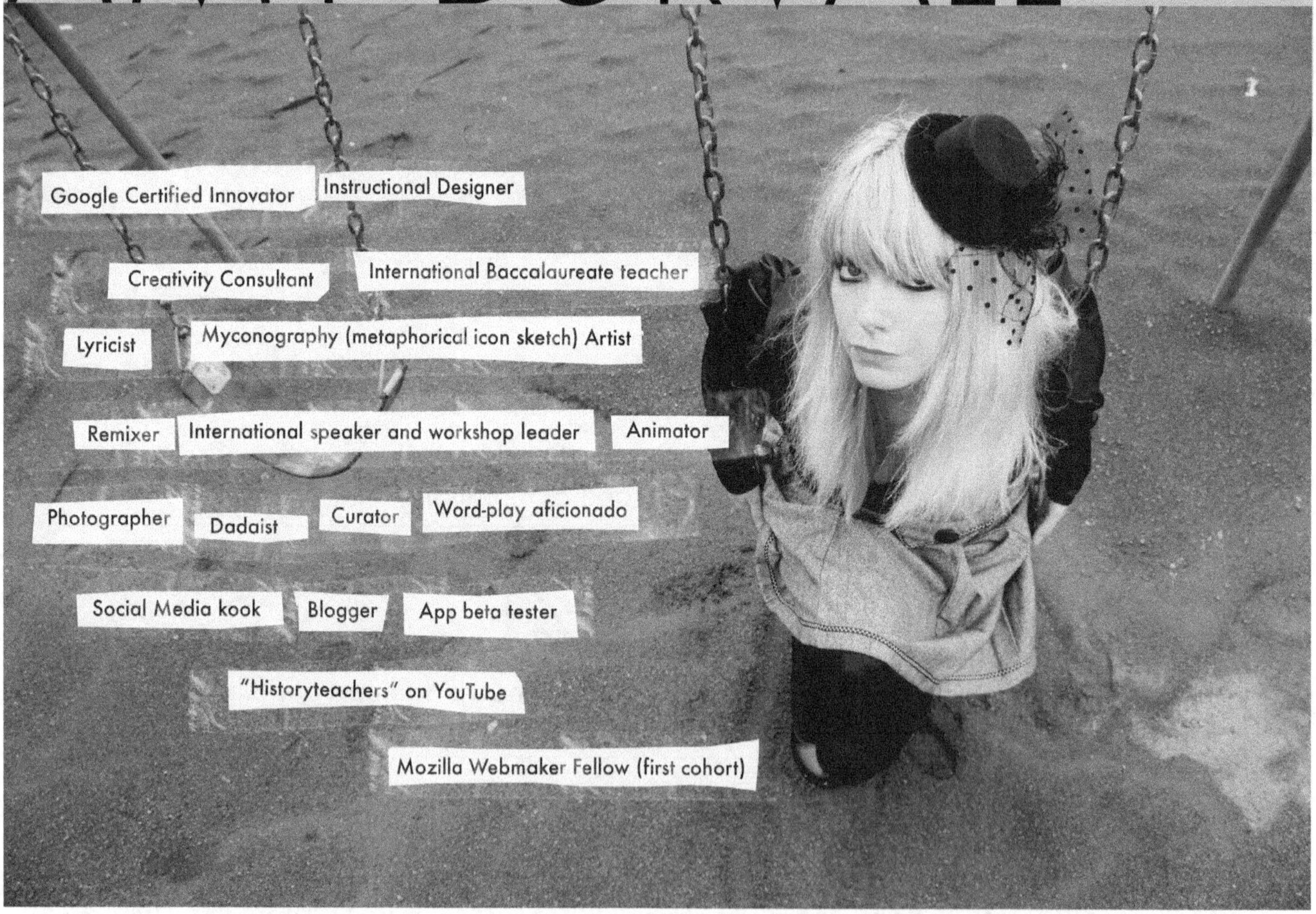

Google Certified Innovator
Instructional Designer
Creativity Consultant
International Baccalaureate teacher
Lyricist
Myconography (metaphorical icon sketch) Artist
Remixer
International speaker and workshop leader
Animator
Photographer
Dadaist
Curator
Word-play aficionado
Social Media kook
Blogger
App beta tester
"Historyteachers" on YouTube
Mozilla Webmaker Fellow (first cohort)

DAN RYDER

Innovation Enthusiast

Improv Comedy Performer & Director

EdCamp Western Maine Co-Founder

Lover of Pop Culture Ephemera

Design Thinking Evangelist

Comic Book Geek

Process Nerd

Generalist

Hybrid Thinker

Podcast Listener

EdTech Advisor

Apple Distinguished Educator

Fueled by Empathy

Hashtag Enthusiast

Blogger

FOREWORD

Creativity is not a "talent," like the ability to run fast. Creativity is what makes us human. Creativity is what makes us happy. And creativity is something you can nurture, expand, grow, and learn. I learned this from my art teacher in the second grade. I went to a very buttoned-down school where children lined up, sat still, and complied with orders and bells. When I objected, I became a troublemaker and misfit. Troublemakers and misfits in my school were often sent to the art teacher, who was the only one willing to put up with us. Fortunately, the art teacher in my school believed that all people are creative, that we all crave and benefit from expressing ourselves creatively, whether it is through the arts or sports or even business. She taught permission, not technique. Thank you, Mrs. Rheingold.

Yes, my art teacher was my mother. But I was far from the only one who benefitted from her approach. When she died at age 99, I wrote a little tribute to her on my website. Soon after, the email started trickling, then flooding in. They all started the same way: "I've been trying to find Mrs. Rheingold for years, but the first time I found her on an Internet search was on your website. She changed the way I look at life and I wanted to thank her." This was forty years after she retired! I tell this story to reinforce the fact that I've thought about creativity—and the potential for teaching it to every person, regardless of whether they think they are "talented"—for many years.

intention

When I first came across Amy Burvall, my first thought was that it was too bad that she would never know my mom because they are kindred spirits. Over the past several years, watching and learning from Amy in multiple media, I've urged her time and again to start teaching creativity. She doesn't just unlock creativity; she overflows with it, bursts with it, liberates it, celebrates it, spreads it infectiously. Teaming with Dan Ryder, another educator whose innovative approach impressed me enough to interview him for the MacArthur Foundation's Digital Media and Learning website, Burvall has finally taken up the challenge. This book is for you, your children, your students, and your teachers. Spread the word—creativity is a birthright.

—Howard Rheingold

author of a dozen books and
former UC Berkeley and
Stanford University professor
rheingold.com

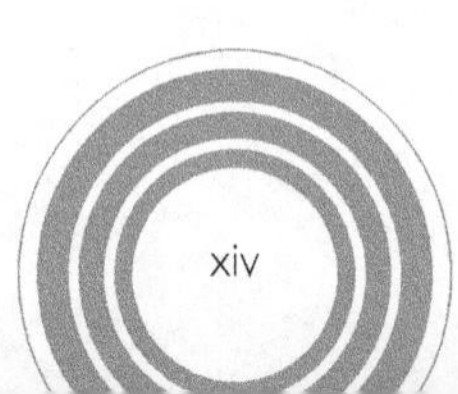

WE DON'T STOP
PLAYING BECAUSE
WE GROW
OLD...
WE GROW
OLD
BECAUSE
WE STOP
PLAYING

GEORGE
BERNARD
SHAW

A LIVING BOOK

Socrates was apprehensive about writing because he knew one couldn't have a conversation with the author, that the written word can "neither defend itself nor come to its own support" (Plato, ***Phaedrus***). Despite this being an analog book, we wholeheartedly hope you will be encouraged to share with us—and the education community at large—your experiences with the activities as you use them in the classroom. You'll find hashtags throughout the book to help you connect with other educators about specific topics. Or, you can always use the hashtags

#IntentiontheBook

and/or

#CriticalCreativity.

We couldn't decide which hashtag we liked better, and then we realized, "It's the Internet! We can have as many as we like!" Use whichever tag feels most comfortable to you, whether it's a specific thought or question related to the book or a notion or inquiry about the marriage of critical thinking and creativity in general.

This is a book about Creativity, so . . .

WHY NO COLOR?

We want to see

YOUR COLORS.

YOUR FONTS.

YOUR HIGHLIGHTS.

YOUR PALETTE.

We want to see this book through YOUR VISION.

That's right, we want you to embrace your inner MEDIEVAL MONK and act as a modern

"ILLUMINATOR"

of this humble manuscript.

So take out your highlighters, felt tips, pencils, or pastels and make this your own. Doodle your notions and mark up the margins. Paraphrase in the perimeters and annotate the empty space. Scribble between the sentences and sticky note over the strategies.

Treat it as the early punk kids treated zines—a sort of DIY embellishment frenzy.

What's more, we'd like you to ***SHARE YOUR REMIXES***

to our #intentionthebook community.

We look forward to seeing your interpretation and insights.

THE INTENTION BEHIND INTENTION

We (Dan and Amy) talk a lot. Actually, we don't talk so much as regularly pepper one another with ideas, suggestions, collaborations, notions, nuggets, morsels, tastes, and promises of something peculiar, whimsical, or otherwise inspiring. We traffic in ideas the way eleven-year-old Dan consumed semi-sweet chocolate chips: with great aplomb and little regard for personal health until the belly hurt or Mom got home, whichever came first.

Of course it isn't "Mom" who taps on the brakes in respect to all that idea consumption but the responsibilities we have to our respective jobs, families, friends, and commitments. Like Dan's sweet mom, those are all good things, but they also mean that, sometimes, the ideas have to wait until we can sneak off for a quick Twitter binge or Instagram snack.

Fortunately, we have both had classrooms where we could turn many of those ideas into action. What we've found, much to our delight, is that these ideas actually push students toward deeper learning and meaningful understanding. What might seem like flights of fancy with hashtags and doodles, mashups and ***portmanteaux***, and cardboard and construction blocks can become pathways for students to use creative expression to demonstrate content knowledge, critical thinking, and the problem solving that will serve them best no matter what their futures may bring.

Portmanteau, a word popularized by Lewis Carroll in ***Through the Looking Glass***, is the French word for "valise." It is used to describe two parts of words merging together and becoming one, just like the two halves of a suitcase.

We call this

CRITICAL CREATIVITY.

Not only are we convinced that creativity is the most essential skill for success in an increasingly unpredictable world, and therefore, "critical," but we also know from experience with our students that ***rich critical thinking*** happens in the process of designing and making.

Critical creativity is **students using creative expression to demonstrate deeper thinking and the nuances of understanding content.**

When students make connections, transform knowledge, and articulate the reasons behind their creative choices, learning becomes more sticky, meaningful, and authentic.

That articulation of creative reasoning is the secret behind the title of this book: **INTENTION.**

We believe in the power of explanation, rationale, and intentionality to elevate our classrooms into places where students shift from passive riders of the rails to active travelers on a quest. Formal education has long been driven by a "because I said so" pedagogy: Authority rests with the few, embodied in the teacher or bound in a textbook. Our current world challenges that hierarchy—we now live in a truly

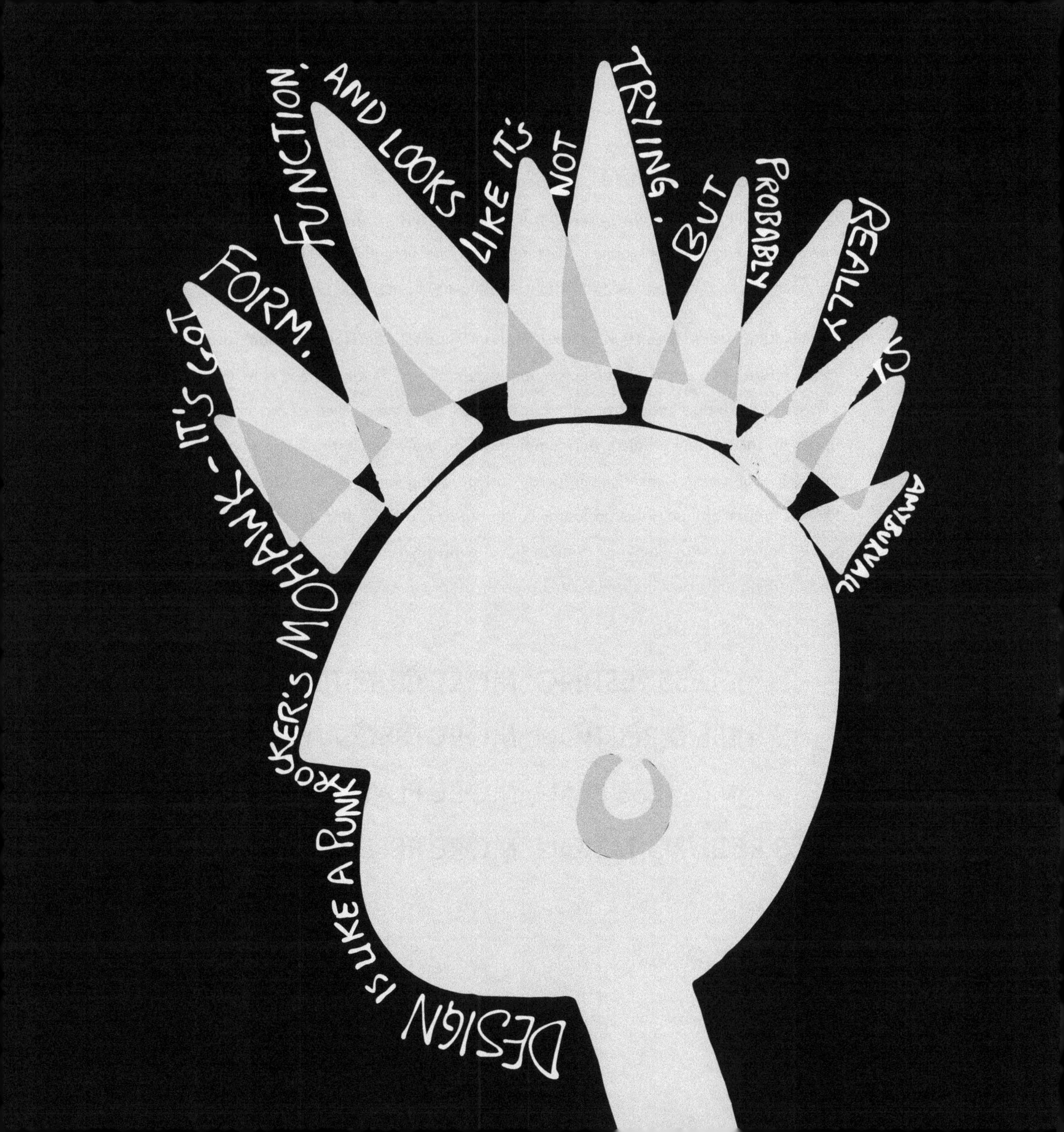

DESIGN IS LIKE A PUNK ROCKER'S MOHAWK – IT'S GOT FORM, FUNCTION, AND LOOKS LIKE IT'S NOT TRYING, BUT PROBABLY REALLY IS.

AMYBUKVIC

participatory culture. Our access to information and ability to create and play with media democratizes the learning landscape. While a classroom of researchers, experts, publishers, and creators may be unfamiliar territory to most, it may actually be a return to our natural inclinations as learners.

We might, as media theorist Marshall McLuhan quipped, ***"be marching backwards to the future,"*** to a world of empiricism, experimentation, DIY, and remix. How might we gain knowledge through questioning and critical thinking, such as the students under the olive tree at Plato's Academy? How do we ***make sense*** from what we take into ***our senses***—tinkering, tugging, and prodding our way to understanding like the master of inquiry-based learning, Leonardo da Vinci? Just as the worlds of work, communication, and information have evolved, our approach to teaching and learning must become one with a greater purpose, mindfulness, and intention. There should be

LESS TESTING, MORE QUESTING

LESS DIRECTION, MORE DISCOVERY

LESS PLAN, MORE PLAY

LESS REGURGITATION, MORE REFLECTION

Challenging students to think in terms of achieving a goal or solving a problem rather than completing an assignment or "getting it done," takes time and persistent patience. It will not happen overnight. There's a culture to be built, one where students will come to expect the learning targets and cognitive skills (the "So what?"), the learning process and products (the "So how?"), and the big takeaways and enduring understandings (the "So why?") to be self-evident.

In the meantime, we make our thinking as clear to those learners as possible through our own transparency and deliberate choice making. We follow author and artist Austin Kleon's chief principle of process: ***Show your work***. We fail with our students, work alongside them to revise the experience, and treat both teaching and learning as a constant exercise in iteration.

We are thrilled you, the reader, are now part of that vision and revision.

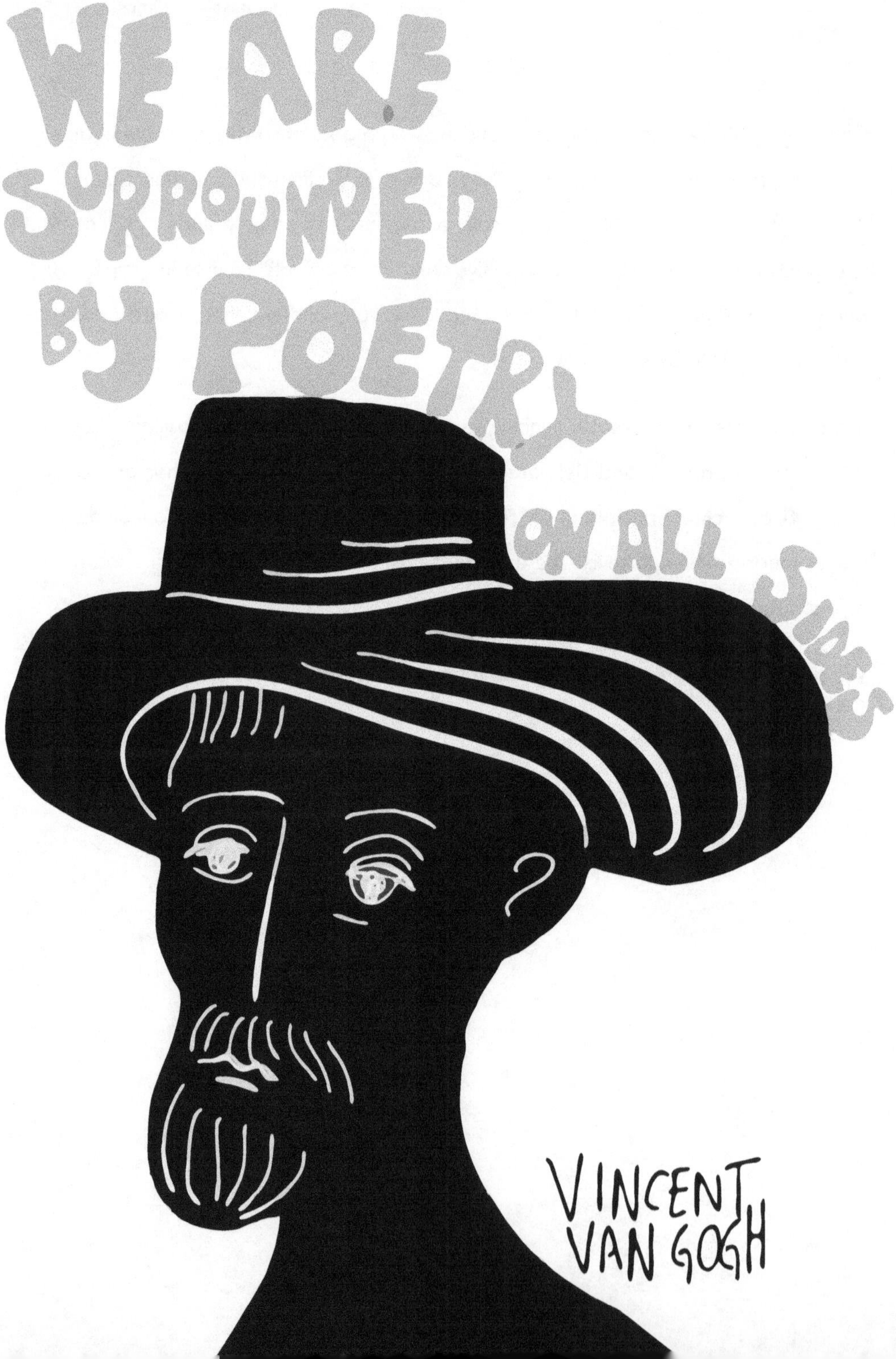

WE ARE SURROUNDED BY POETRY ON ALL SIDES

VINCENT VAN GOGH

CREATIVITY CREDO
(WHAT WE BELIEVE)

Creativity is a birthright.

We are all born with creative impulses. Although we all vary in "talent," we can train ourselves to be more creative by understanding how creativity works, by practicing divergent thinking strategies, and by worrying less about right and wrong while caring more about playing and exploring—two of our most basic instincts.

Creativity is a tao.

Creativity is a way of thinking, being, and doing—a ***tao***. It's a lens through which we experience a richer world. It's about using unexpected mediums and repurposing that which would be cast aside to develop something new. Creativity may evolve in its purpose and appearance, yet it remains a pathway to understanding and problem solving.

Creativity is connecting disparate dots ... and we must grow our dots.

Creativity is about seeing relationships which others fail to see, forcing juxtapositions between the unexpected. It's playful and often stems from whimsy, tinkering, and humor. And while inquiry and experiential learning is sticky, direct instruction and guided learning (both with formal and informal pathways) are necessary because that is how we grow our dots in order to make connections. These metaphorical dots are bits of knowledge and experience we've gathered and stored over time. Creativity in education, then, is a balance of curating ("dot collection"), finding, sense making, and associating.

Creativity has lineage.

All creative work is derivative and built upon the ruins and triumphs of the past. Nothing is truly novel; Everything is a mashup or remix, including ourselves! What we absorb into our lives—the people, books, films, music—makes us who we are. Creative work reflects our selected influences. Respect and acknowledge the work's creative heritage, as well as that of the creator, and always, always give attribution.

Creativity thrives on context: time, trust, and tools.

Fostering creativity means providing an environment conducive to creative, playful thinking and making. The environment is both physical and psychological. Trust and respect in the social setting are imperative. The concepts of ***mise-en-scène*** (setting the scene) and ***mise en place*** (having tools at the ready) help us think about the physical environment. Mobile technology and a resurgent respect for another mobile technology, journaling, doodling, and sketching, means our studios can be anywhere at any time—so long as we are willing to trust ourselves to try.

Creativity craves constraints.

The way out of the "box" is via the shackles. Creativity works best with prompts, parameters, and limitations. Too much freedom is daunting and inhibiting. We flourish with conditions, rules, and challenges. While we can develop constraints, serendipity and chance also work as an inspiration.

Creative thinking and being are the skills of the century.

The need for cognitive agility and flexibility is ever increasing in our uncertain and exponentially changing world. We need to be chameleons who can learn, unlearn, and relearn anew. When we are able to remix a concept, we have truly learned it. Thus, all learning should involve some aspect of creativity—whether it be thinking about something differently or making something tangible to bring life to knowledge. Education should inspire us to want to wonder and learn about things on our own. It should point us in the direction of tools (hardware, software, and mindware) that we can use to facilitate our lifelong learning pursuits.

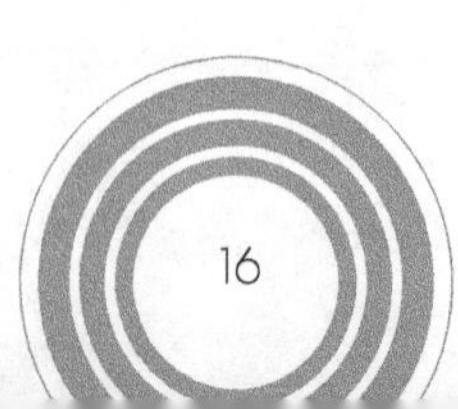

ALMOST
ALL
CREATIVITY
INVOLVES
PURPOSEFUL
PLAY
ABRAHAM
MASLOW

ANATOMY OF CRITICAL CREATIVITY: HOW TO USE THIS BOOK

The What and the Why

The first half of ***Intention*** digs deep into the reason and the why behind our approach to teaching and learning through critical creativity. We define the terms. We provide the philosophical underpinnings. We wax poetic. If you want to better understand the madness to our methodology, come here first.

In these chapters, you will discover the language and terminology we have appropriated or coined for ourselves. You will also read stories and anecdotes from our past and our most recent present. And, if all goes according to plan, you'll "get" critical creativity and see as we see it: an opportunity to wield creative expression as a mighty tool for demonstrating understanding. Here's a quick chapter-by-chapter breakdown of this section:

Chapter 1

Making Meaning:
If They Build It, They Will Get It

We outline the value of creativity to the process of making meaning and developing understanding, both central components of authentic literacy.

Chapter 2

Chutzpah and Whimsy, Content and Clarity:
Taking Chances on Imagination

We explain how to better foster the relationship between imagination and content and explore the inherent value of purposeful play.

Chapter 3

No Dumpster Projects:
Transforming Flights of Fancy into Pathways to Authenticity

We lay out a process for getting from idea to product, building the layers of critical thinking and intentionality that better ensure the work students do matters.

THE HOW

The second half of Intention features critical-creativity activities, experiences, and assessments we believe *any teacher in any content* area can adopt to suit the classroom's needs.

Although the ideas we share have been structured around typical middle and high school academic outcomes, expectations, and cognitive demands, elementary teachers will find inspiration within these pages as well. Feel free to remix, mash up, or transform anything and everything found herein.

The ideas you'll find in this section are organized in a catalog format for easy reference. We have compiled forty-two opportunities to bring critical creativity into the classroom, categorizing them into six general themes: Words, Images, Sounds, Body, Stuff, and Social Media. These are not tight little silos (most every catalog entry could easily be placed in two more categories), but we've found that a little structure can go a long way toward making the unfamiliar accessible to educators and students alike.

Each catalog entry features the following components to help navigate the critical creativity waters.

TITLE.

'Nuff said.

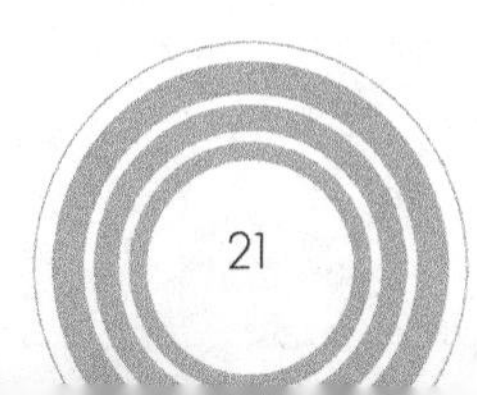

HASHTAG.

Media scholar Derrick de Kerckhove once identified the hashtag (officially known as an "octothorpe") as the **"soul of the Internet"** (*The Augmented Mind*). It has become social media's democratizing superhero, able to transcend barriers of geography and familiarity in favor of affinity, connecting participants with similar interests from across the globe. After meeting briefly in person at SXSWEdu several years ago, we really got to know one another by sharing our work on Twitter and Instagram. Thus, we forged our friendship on social media and invite you to join us online. To facilitate connection and idea sharing, we have included ***a specific tag for each exercise*** (as well as a hashtag for the book itself). Use the hashtag on social media to show your work. Likewise, use the HASHTAG when you pose questions or comments that build upon ideas and post pictures of planning and classrooms in progress. Use it anytime to connect with a growing community of educators who are looking to bring more critical creativity and intention into the classroom.

TARGET.

Here, you will find a basic description of the catalog entry, what students can be expected to create, the tools they will use, and the essential critical-thinking skills being assessed by the entry's exercise. Also included here are any creative constraints or challenging boundaries within which students must operate in order to heighten the experience outlined in the entry.

Because knowledge and comprehension-level thinking skills tend to be more universally evident in content-area classrooms, we tend to focus the TARGET on lower-order critical-thinking skills in order to help educators see the possibilities of applying critical-creativity experiences to their classrooms. Worry not, the deeper thinking is coming.

PATHWAY.

In each PATHWAY, section, we describe one possible approach to crafting a classroom lesson around this particular critical-creativity experience. We deliberately call this a PATHWAY rather than identify it as a set of instructions or rules. The PATHWAYS we present are only a few of the many viable ways to go about getting from start to finish. We encourage you to modify and adjust these suggestions to suit your own particular styles and needs.

Over the space of each PATHWAY, there are often variables identified and options one might choose. Progressing along each step, we hope educators start to see the evolution of thinking skills move from the lower to the higher order by the time **students are explaining their intentions** behind each creation.

TAKEAWAY.

The TAKEAWAY section highlights the higher-order thinking and bigger-picture understandings students will develop. While the discrete content knowledge and comprehension is certainly important, we believe these TAKEAWAYS truly justify critical creativity being worth the time it takes.

APPLICATION.

We present at least three different ways to apply each catalog entry to content-area learning. Across the catalog, you will find APPLICATIONS for science, health, math, and world languages integration in addition to our English and social studies wheelhouses. Critical creativity has a home well beyond the humanities, and APPLICATION shows exactly that.

AMPLIFICATION.

Using "yes, and" allows us to take a simple idea to another, brighter, bolder level. AMPLIFICATION suggestions show you how to elevate the catalog entries into deeper-learning experiences for students. Often these amplifications involve authentic audiences and sometimes they involve real-world problem solving.

LEVERAGING THE LEXICON

Without a vocabulary, it might be difficult to see how this book functions or to self-assess your own comfort and experience with creativity in the classroom. It's much like when an English teacher lacking any semblance of automotive repair skills tries to explain what's wrong with his '98 Corolla to his mechanic. Said educator might just as well say, "The red light is on. It's got 200,000 miles on it. Do whatever you gotta do to keep it running for another year. Call me when it's ready."

To articulate our observations and understandings, we need the words and terminology for those observations and understandings. The following are concepts that serve as the foundation of this book and guide each of the activities in the catalog.

INTENTION, EVIDENCE, AND EDUSYMBIOSIS

Intention sits at the heart of critical creativity. No matter how clever, witty, beautiful, or delightful a product may be, if it is purely the result of circumstance, it cannot serve as effective evidence of understanding. As educators, we must all ask questions such as, ***How might we layer intention upon itself?*** and, ***How can we help students see every step in the creative process as an opportunity to demonstrate learning?*** The reality is that aesthetic choices, creative media, and delivery method all have the potential to signify content knowledge. We need to hold students accountable for evidence of their understanding, for their creative decisions, and for their growth.

> "The medium is the message."
> —Marshall McLuhan

We've found that when intention, creativity, and content intersect, students often deliver work that exceeds the standards. For example, when students create soundtracks for an epic poem, the close reading and semantic connections they first make between lyric, sound, and dramatic verse fuel confidence in their understanding. That confidence then translates over into the means by which they showcase their knowledge, and there it is once again: **edusymbiosis**—creativity informing content, informing creativity, collectively demonstrating deeper understanding.

RIGOROUS WHIMSY AND REMIX

Playful creativity and unfettered artistic exploration have their place. We need not align every minute and moment in the classroom to a standard. However, too often, creative experiences in the classroom send us down pathways that delight, amuse, and entertain without ever demonstrating deeper learning. **Rigorous whimsy** calls upon greater intentionality with creative expression, to challenge students to leverage the seemingly trivial into the substantially meaningful. Stop-motion animated Oreo cookies demonstrate geometric principles, while carefully arranged LEGO minifigures may illustrate character development; thoughtfully designed dinner parties mimic historical timelines, and purposefully crafted hashtags can relate the scientific method.

> "All ideas are secondhand, consciously and unconsciously drawn from a million outside sources."
>
> —**Mark Twain**

Discovering opportunities for rigorous whimsy becomes easy when we accept the assertion by documentary filmmaker and media critic, Kirby Ferguson, that **"everything is remix."** Every lesson and activity, every routine and assessment comes from the graceful collision of context and content. We take the successes and failures of the past and recombine them with the strengths and needs of the present. This how we grow as educators: twisting our prior work into new and unexpected arrangements and then applying the results to the problem at hand. Remix mindset allows us to gather inspiration and create learning experiences for our students, pulling from diverse sources—Maria Popova's ***Brain Pickings*** blog (brainpickings.org), the pages of ***Wired*** magazine, Austin Kleon's Twitter feed, and Brandon Stanton's "Humans of New York" on Instagram (humansofnewyork.com).

MASHUPS AND METAPHORS

Sometimes those graceful collisions take on a more explosive quality, resulting in less a remix and more a **mashup**—taking pieces of this and that, shaping them into new and unexpected arrangements, and applying the results to the problem at hand. This process is how our culture evolves—an iPod is a Walkman mashed up with a computer; a Walkman, a transistor radio mashed up with a tape deck; a tape deck, a reel-to-reel mashed-up with a stereo, and so forth. In the same way, we fuse haiku and iconography into visual poetry, smash root words into new technical language, and combine dance with history to tell stories in rhythmic time.

Mashups thrive in comparison with the juxtaposition of two works opening meaningful pathways toward understanding each. However, a comparison need not always result in a mashup. Thinking in analogy, drawing parallels, and building extended **metaphors** all require meaningful connections. And those connections come from deeper connections, every layer of dots connecting until tiers of webbed understanding emerges.

SERENDIPITY AND CRYPTOMNESIA

Sometimes all of the moving parts in the universe fall into sync and everything just ... clicks.

You cannot plan for serendipity, though you can foster cultures of creativity, collaboration, content, and collisions.

Out of such conditions, the seemingly random emerges as the sublimely intentional, especially when students take the time to analyze and unpack the moment. Serendipitous moments grant a pause. ***How did this experience come to pass?*** Upon reflection, you realize a bias toward intentional creation and cooperative exploration prepares students for these moments all along.

With the sheer volume of content and ideas circulating our cultural landscapes, it becomes more and more likely that your ideas, and those of your students, are influenced by past readings, viewings, and listenings—even if you cannot place the precise source.

> "Whether you THINK or you BELIEVE or you KNOW, you're a lot of other people ... but the moment you FEEL ... you're nobody but yourself."
>
> —**e e cummings**

Cryptomnesia occurs when you (or your students) have an idea that you believe is wholly unique and original; you truly have no recollection that it has been informed by another's creation. Some refer to this phenomenon as an unaware plagiarism, casting a negative light on its byproducts. But what if cryptomnesia served as testimony to the power of the subconscious, the importance of introducing students to creative expression in all of its forms, and the value of curating—and teaching students to curate—high-quality content to explore? Were educators to nurture students' ability to trace the lineage of their thinking, those moments of creative amnesia could become opportunities for **celebration and homage** rather than criticism and embarrassment.

> **"It's not where you take things from, it's where you take them to."**
>
> **—Jean-Luc Godard**

LINEAGE AND LEGACY

To know our roots is to understand our present and inform our future. Attribution leads to inspiration. You must delve into the derivation of creativity, the influences and ideas that came before. As you explore both the revered and the forgotten works of the past, you and your students will experience the excitement of something new. And as students build respect for where big ideas come from, they should also explore where ***their*** ideas come from, tracing the lineage of their own creative spirits and the intellectual genealogy of their work.

How might students leave their own marks? How might their demonstration of content knowledge take the form of creative content? How might their assessments live outside the moment and beyond the classroom? We live in an era where building a **legacy** is as simple as a blog, as easy as Instagram, or as effortless as a tweet. An eye to the future could mean the difference between an assignment and authenticity.

> **"Creative works may indeed be a kind of property, but it's property we are all building on."**
>
> **—Kirby Ferguson**

EMPATHY AND AGENCY

Empathy asks us to see through the eyes of another. It is not about feeling sympathy or pity; it is about understanding another's point of view and the reasons underlying that perspective. Growing students' capacity for empathy results in better problem-solving skills; those who put others' needs ahead of their own tend to find more success. The "it's good enough for me" game takes a sideline when students take on different roles and perspectives. Empathetic students become better attuned to finding alternative solutions, adopting new angles, and seeing the situation from different sets of eyes.

Educators benefit when we empathize with students and afford them greater agency. Critical creativity thrives when students feel empowered to make meaningful choices, to apply their experience and knowledge, to be trusted with their own success, and to struggle. This is not to suggest educators toss our hands in the air and let the wild rumpus begin. Students want and need direction and guidance, rules, and limitations. How might educators collaborate with students to establish those frameworks? And how might those efforts result in a learning environment more akin to an artist's studio than a classroom stereotype?

CREATIVE CONSTRAINTS AND IDEA AMPLIFICATION

There is a beautiful place where balance between control and creativity yields sublime results. Creative constraints challenge students to innovate new uses for familiar materials, to simulate workplace limitations of budgets and deadlines, and to discover the power they have to exercise their talents and abilities in any situation.

> **"Art consists in limitation. The most beautiful part of every picture is the frame."**
>
> **—G.K. Chesterton**

Creative constraints lead to solutions and notions worth sharing and exploring further, for precisely that reason: The solutions emerged from boundaries. Such solutions provide proof of authentic understanding and learning that persists beyond a study session or a testing date.

Idea amplification occurs when students put their ideas out into the world, with the intent of reaching an audience that may then inform its own work with these solutions and then apply the ideas to new contexts. As educators, we can be satisfied with the classroom learning—or we can take it further. We can end with the content knowledge—or we can explore its relevance and value to the world beyond the school. Our hope is that you will challenge students to develop ideas that have a scope that reaches far beyond the classroom.

> **"If your work isn't online, it doesn't exist."**
>
> **—Austin Kleon**

KNOWING
IS
NOT
ENOUGH
- WE MUST
APPLY
... WE
MUST DO
LEONARDO DA VINCI

CONSTRAINTS

REMIX

FRAMES

CONSTANT FLUX

agility

Content Agnostic

CONNECT THE DOTS

PROCESS

LIMITATIONS

mise-en-scène; mise en place

CHAPTER 1

MAKING MEANING

IF THEY BUILD IT THEY WILL GET IT

The PROCESS of CREATING engages the modalities and deepens the process of UNDERSTANDING.

CRITICAL CREATIVITY grows from COMPLEX connections, not from receiving and regurgitating.

CONTENT and CREATIVITY are not mutually exclusive.

"I have the answers

to the questions

they never ask."

—Gwenivere Burvall,
age 11

"Creativity" as a concept often seems daunting. Many people feel they aren't "creative" when perhaps they really mean they don't believe themselves to be particularly ***artistically talented.*** Creativity, however, is much broader than any brushstroke—it's a way of thinking and doing. And creativity, like anything else, is something anyone can learn about, practice, and become better at.

Each idea offered in this book can help cultivate creative ***capacities*** in students. They are not discipline-specific and can be adapted to any curriculum. After all,

creativity is content agnostic.

Perhaps the greatest calling of an educator is to

inspire students to want to wonder and learn about things on their own.

Fulfilling that calling requires that you

point students in the direction of tools

(hardware, software, and *mindware*) that they can use to facilitate their respective (lifelong) learning pursuits. One perception of our responsibility as educators is to prepare the youth under our influence for ***"the future."*** But, in light of our increasingly disappointing lack of time-travel abilities, we must, in this matter, turn to the affirmations of Yoda:

IMPOSSIBLE TO SEE... THE FUTURE IS...

One thing we can do is pay close attention to the now, and we can acknowledge that, at present, technology has overwhelmingly changed the way we work. We are moving rapidly to a ***creative economy***—one that is fluid and flexible and requires workers to constantly shift roles and positions. That demand for flexibility means we must all—teacher and student alike—be committed to learning and creating constantly. With increased automation of tasks, those with an edge will be the ones who do work that ***leverages our humanity***. Unfortunately, cultivating the **essence of being human**—developing a sense of wonder and beauty, persistent curiosity, creative thinking, self-awareness, compassion, and empathy—too often falls by the wayside in today's schools and workplaces.

> **"True teachers are those who use themselves as bridges over which they invite their students to cross—then, having facilitated their crossing, joyfully collapse, encouraging them to CREATE THEIR OWN."**
>
> **—Nikos Kazantzakis**

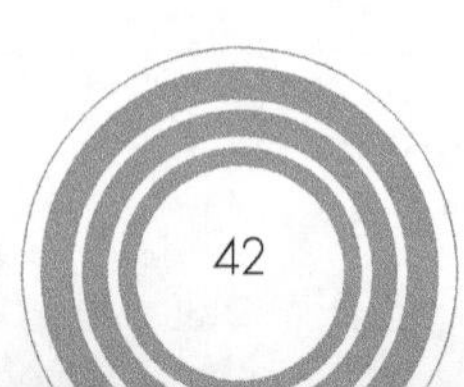

THE PROCESS OF CREATING ENGAGES THE MODALITIES AND DEEPENS THE PROCESS OF UNDERSTANDING

If we are truthful with ourselves, we'll admit that a lot of what we "learned" as youth is fairly obsolete now. (Think of the hours you spent learning how to navigate through the Dewey decimal system, memorize phone numbers, or how to write a proper check.) Children today will be cast into an **adulthood of constant flux**. Even now, there is an exponential increase in the speed at which some skills and knowledge are becoming "obsolete." One of the best traits to have, therefore, is

agility: a chameleon-like talent to quickly adapt to a new environment with new demands.

Being able to learn, unlearn, and relearn anew is imperative. Nobel Prize-winning author **Doris Lessing** defines "learning" as the moment you "***suddenly understand something you've understood all your life, but in a new way***." Indeed, when you are able to remix a concept, you have truly learned it. Thus, all learning should involve some aspect of creativity—whether it be thinking about something differently, holding an idea askew, or making something tangible to bring life to knowledge.

Think of a Skateboarder.

How does he learn a new trick? He finds out about it (usually by observing another, more advanced skater) and then tries to emulate it. Rarely does a skater land a new trick on the first try—indeed, it requires hours of practice and repeated falls. The lovely thing about skateboarders, by the way, is that they tend to have an ***intrinsic desire*** to improve and work at their sport. We could all take a lesson about **personal learning paths** from them. They are internally motivated and committed to learning—even when it means enduring physical pain!

Let's say our skateboarder perfects the trick and can replicate it exactly. Yes, we can say he has "learned it"; he has memorized the technique, gone through the motions enough times to **internalize it** (perhaps even with some "muscle memory"), and **understands when** the move should be employed (for example, on this surface, but not that one).

But wait—what happens next? He riffs on that move, adds to it, tweaks it. Skateboarding is a lot like jazz. Learning takes place in a highly social setting, where each person responds to what the environment throws at them (think empty swimming pools, park benches, handrails!) and adapts as necessary.

In search of constant innovation, skaters see value in changing up what they've learned and developing something new.

They continually harness their ability to **change, remix, distort, embellish, improve upon, and tweak**.

This is the crux of learning.

Learning Is Creativity. Creativity Is Remix.

If a student can, like the skateboarder, **demonstrate an understanding of the nuances** of an existing piece of knowledge—so much that she can, in fact, remix it and fashion it into something novel—then she has indeed learned it.

How might we, as educators, offer students the chance to not simply encounter, memorize, reiterate, and or perform "knowledge," but to **truly use knowledge in new ways?**

CRITICAL CREATIVITY GROWS FROM COMPLEX CONNECTIONS, NOT FROM RECEIVING AND REGURGITATING

Creativity inherently involves remix and "connecting the dots."

These metaphorical dots are bits of knowledge and experience that have been gathered and stored over time.

The "dots" are all over the place, and

it's often necessary to reach into the depths of

the mind's closets to retrieve them.

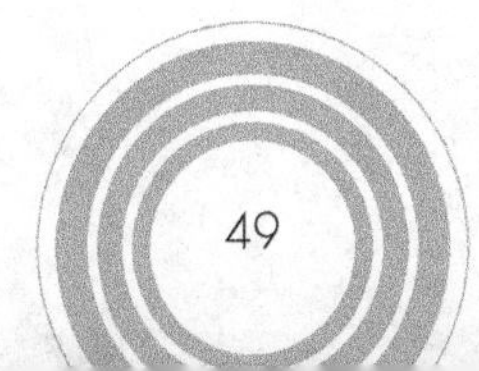

intention

Much is learned in school, but students increasingly seek learning outside of traditional settings, in so-called **"affinity spaces"** made possible by the Internet and social media. This dot connecting takes practice. It's a balance of curating ("dot collection"), and making sense of and associating information bits. Partaking in "**combinatorial play**," as Einstein deemed it, should be part of our training. To Einstein, combinatorial play was the essence of a productive thinking process. Indeed, the word "cognition" is derived from the Latin *"cognito,"* which translates to *"know together."* That *"co-"* is important—humans ideate like LEGO bricks. The key is to combine and recombine ideas, images, and concepts into multitudinous mashups, eventually honing in on something novel. Often this means pairing things that don't conventionally belong together—a sort of "blind date" for thoughts.

Creativity as a concept is frequently misunderstood. If we are talking about dot connecting, then we must acknowledge that all creative work is derivative—that everything is built upon the ruins of the past. **We all, as Isaac Newton mused, "*stand on the shoulders of giants.*"**

It is crucial to identify one's own creative influences and acknowledge them. Author, illustrator, and idea-trafficker Austin Kleon lays out an entire manifesto for such in his fantastic book, ***Steal Like an Artist***. (You ought to put your hands on a copy, posthaste!) As consumers and creatives, we all need the skill of being able to deconstruct a work and trace its **creative lineage**. When students dismantle a pop song into its influences, into the sources of its rhythms and melodies, into the background behind its writers and performers, into the process of its production and popularity, they gain an appreciation of what came before, as well as a realization that the past is truly prologue. If pop-dance-punk band Panic! at the Disco were not students of their craft, their 2016 release, "Crazy = Genius" would otherwise not exist. Legendary Beach Boy, songwriter, and producer Brian Wilson serves as titular and lyrical inspiration for the track. Wilson's body of work, which layers in sounds upon sounds and applies string and brass arrangements to pop-psychedelia, clearly influences Panic!'s multi-textured sound on this cut, as well as others. In acknowledging their influences, Panic! at the Disco is not derivative or flirting with plagiarism. Instead, the band is educating its audience and freeing its own creative constraints to pull from a far wider range of sounds to suit its purposes, whether it be the beat of tympani drums or a lyric from Verdi.

Students must be taught the value of providing attribution when appropriating even the smallest elements. In the words of French cinema icon Jean-Luc Godard:

"It's not where you take things from —it's where you take them to."

The idea that schools need "more creativity" is as readily agreed to as if it were a request for "more paper clips" or "more coffee filters." But, like any nuanced facet of being human, true learning and creativity are not that formulaic. Is anyone—are *you*—willing to take the time to understand **how creativity works** and to figure out **how to do it?** We hope so. Because creativity doesn't just happen.

A major misconception about creativity is that it's about ***freedom***. There is nothing more frustrating than having open-ended chaos—no rules or conditions. Amy's mother, a primary-school teacher, used to say that kids crave boundaries so much that they will push into mid-air seeking out a wall. Humans long for these metaphorical walls because they mean safety and security. If you have ever stared at a blank page wondering what to write, you know the feeling. That is why journals with prompts are so successful. It's the same reason photo challenges or hashtag games on Twitter are always popular. While few people want an activity or task to be over-prescribed, **conditions, rules, challenges, and design "specs"** create opportunities to thrive. The presence of parameters that shape a creative task actually makes a person ***more creative.***

G.K. Chesterton said so brilliantly:

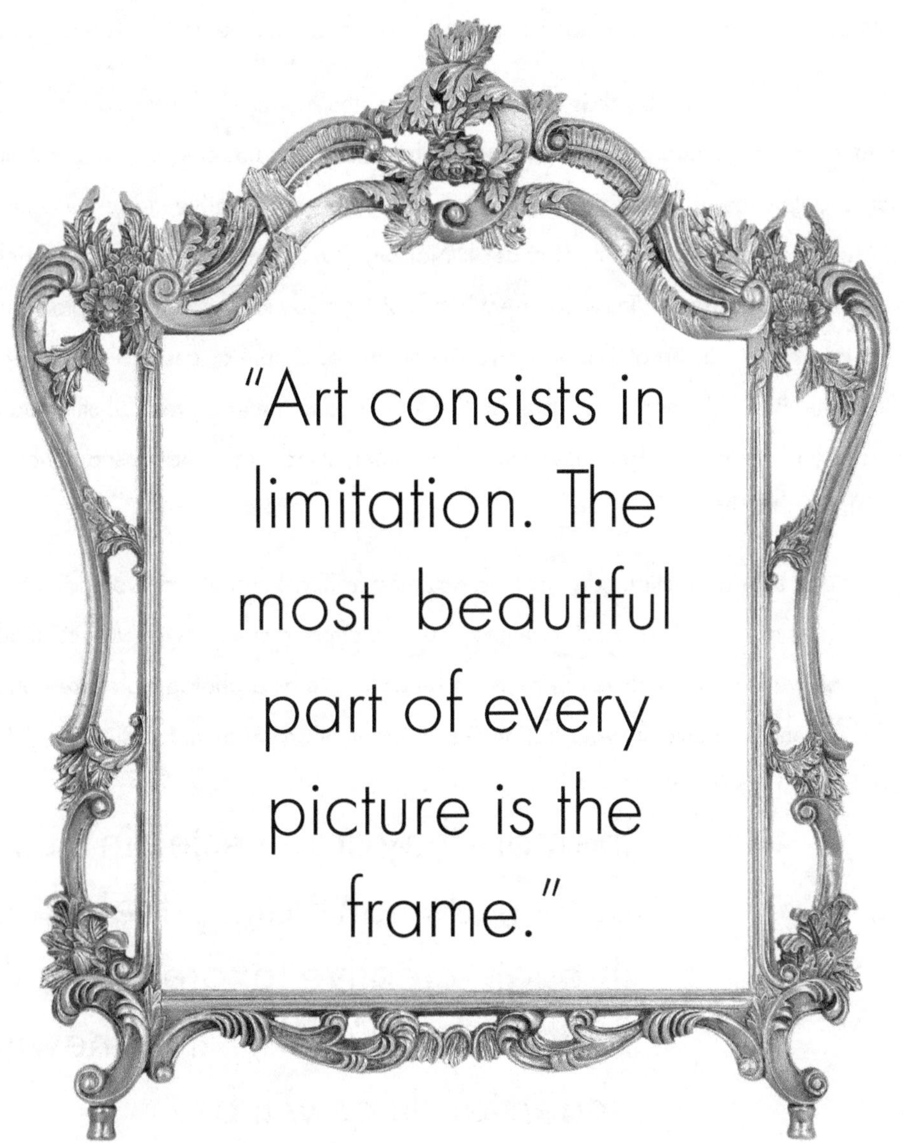

That is the ***raison d'être*** for this book: We wanted to share recipes of creative constraints that have worked well in our classrooms and in our personal creative journeys.

While the focus of this book is cognitive (that is, the exercises described tease out student knowledge and understanding through making), it is undeniable that creativity itself is quite visceral. There is a special feeling you get when you've made something yourself. Harvard researchers Michael I. Norton, Daniel Mochon, and Dan Ariely identified this feeling as "The Ikea Effect." Their 2011 study showed that people value what they make—a sort of "labor = love" mentality. As simple as assembling a piece of Ikea furniture is (note the sarcasm), it (the process and the end product) still means more to you emotionally because of the "DIY" element than if you had just purchased a prefabricated item.

This kind of self-satisfaction can apply to anything from a question you've posed to a community, a piece of digital storytelling you've crafted, a solution you've designed, or an innovation you've developed. It can be as simple as a photograph taken on a travel adventure to an outfit your daughter puts together on her own. For students, "The Ikea Effect" means that

the more they are invested in their learning and in demonstrating their knowledge through creative expression, the more relevant and "sticky" their newly formed understandings will be.

IKEA

Mise-en-Scène; Mise en Place.

In stagecraft, the design aspects of a production—the setting up of the space—is called ***mise-en-scène.*** A thoughtful approach to the environment is imperative if students are going to feel comfortable and grow in creative confidence. Cultivating a **community of trust and a playful atmosphere** is conducive to critical creativity.

Students should be encouraged to run with their curiosity, feel at ease in a state of questioning, take in different perspectives, examine things from all angles, challenge assumptions, and actively listen. They must be self-aware in order to defend their own creative reasoning and design choices. Likewise, they must be respectful so that they may appreciate the same articulation from peers.

Another concept nicked from the world outside education is ***mise en place.*** This is chef's terminology for "everything in its place" or "at the ready." A space prepped with the needed tools for making (such as art supplies, index cards, or cameras) and remixing (like old magazines, newspapers, or LEGO bricks) not only facilitates creativity, but often ***inspires*** it. For each activity in this book and in the "Supply Closet" (page 318), we provide suggestions for stimulating materials that will become your go-to design kit. It is important to achieve ***fluency*** with one's creativity—that is, knowing which tool to use and **when** and **why** you opted for that tool (this applies not only to creating work, but for sharing that work as well). Any good fan of philosopher and futurist Marshall McLuhan will know that the ***"medium is the message."*** Part of the ***Intention*** process is holding students accountable for explaining the choices they make as they create.

Ask . . .

"Why did you choose this font? Why did you use these colors?"

"Why did you make a poster rather than another product?"

"Tell us a story about your process of creating this. Where did you run into difficulties, and when did it feel fantastic?"

"What were you hoping to accomplish with this design feature?"

"What do you want your audience to take away from this?"

"What were your intentions behind these choices?"

CONTENT AND CREATIVITY ARE NOT MUTUALLY EXCLUSIVE

Art is science. Art is math. Art is English and social studies, language, and health. Evolution proves a beautiful metamorphosis over time. Palindromes possess gorgeous symmetry. Poetry sculpts text into shape, "I Have a Dream" pulses with cadence, Spanish trills from the tongue, and the human body remains an exceptional study in mixed media.

Creative exploration and content learning are not mutually exclusive enterprises. In fact, they **inform one another** and share a rather glorious symbiotic relationship.

To create art, one must know something of the essential qualities of ***both the subject*** being captured ***and the medium*** through which one is expressing those qualities. What follows are just a few examples of how content learning combines with creative exploration to better ensure ideas stick around for the long term, avoiding the "know it for the test then kick it into the trash" default setting for which far too many students are famous. In the catalog section of this book, you'll find more uses and strategies for applying each of these concepts in the classroom.

DOODLES

Consider a doodle, the most rarefied, "simplistic" of hand-drawn visual expressions. (Better yet, read Sunni Brown's ***The Doodle Revolution*** or Mike Rohde's ***The Sketchnote Handbook***.) An effective doodle requires the creator to break down a subject—a house, a cow, a marshmallow, a 1940's Ford pick-up—into its most simple and recognizable features. Then the creator must compose those features in ink, crayon, graphite, or pixels in such a way that a single glance is all it takes for the viewer to identify the subject. The more the creator ***knows the subject, the audience, and the medium***, the more likely that little doodle may carry weight and meaning and prove its utility in new contexts. That doodle might show up in notebooks and margins, on marker boards and Instagram posts, and be recognized. That doodle can be used for ***concrete, literal*** purposes and for ***abstract, metaphorical*** tasks. To a few folks, it may just be a circle with a stack of three horizontal lines beneath and a few diagonal lines radiating above. But for many others, it is an idea that persists no matter when or where encountered. That solidification of an idea makes this simple art form a powerful tool with which you can equip students, which is why we use it in several of the exercises you'll find in this book.

VOLLEY

The relationship between knowledge and art can also be seen in our affinity for ***#hashtaggerie***, a term of endearment we invented for our collaborative social media volley (page 287). Here's how it works for us: Dan sends Amy a whimsical hashtag, which Amy then illustrates in her trademark style. Amy in turn sends original doodles to Dan, for which he must compose an appropriately whimsical hashtag.

One of our favorites is #NarwhalianWarholians, a fusion of pop-art deity and oceanic mammalia. Dan sent Amy the hashtag based on a few criteria. One, Dan knew Amy has fascination with Andy Warhol. Two, Dan knew Amy's daughter was going through an intense narwhal-loving period at the time. (At the time of printing, it was unclear whether she had fully recovered.) Three, Dan knew alliteration sticks; the bounce of the internal rhyme in this hashtag makes it particularly resonant. Four, and most importantly, Dan knows Warhol's work in pop art, that narwhals are essentially sea unicorns, that the prevalent unicorn imagery in the pop culture of the moment was not altogether unlike the ubiquitous Marilyn or Campbell's soup presence of Warhol's world, and that the potential was there for Amy to make something magical. Similarly, Amy knew that to distill Warhol down to his white mop top and glasses would make the image immediately recognizable, the juxtaposition of rotund whale to slight artist would make it that much more playful, and the concrete visual to complement the wordplay would leave a lasting impression.

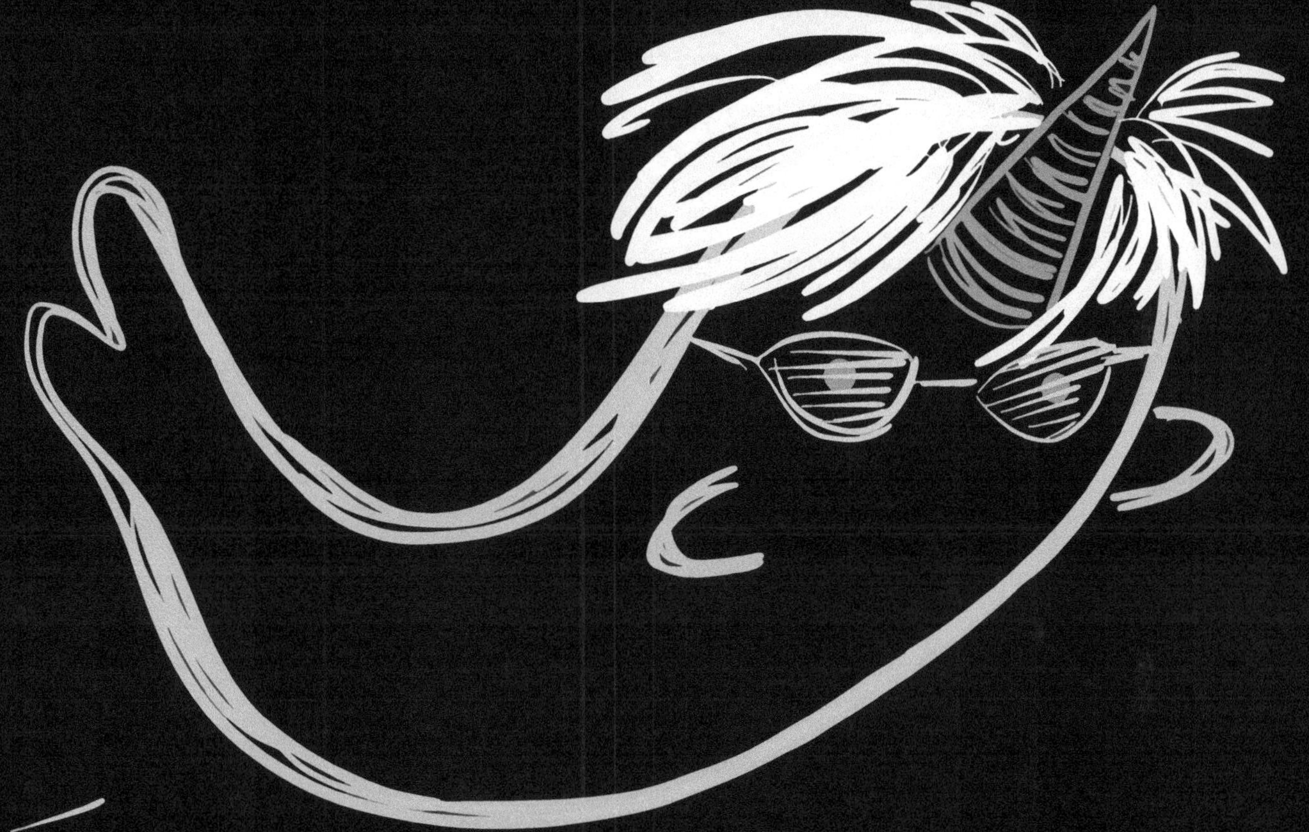

04
06
15

#NARWALIANWARHOLIANS

Imagine asking students to collaborate with a fellow classmate, a younger student (seniors and kindergarteners make great pairs), or someone from another school. Using the #hashtaggerie example, one student could construct a whimsically worded tagged phrase to contextualize a bit of a novel, a current event, a philosophical movement, or a scientific discovery. Another student could sketch, using as much metaphorical iconography as he can muster. Or, perhaps the first student uses photography to capture the spirit of a poem she is studying or a concept in geometry—the partner could remix the photo with artistic edits, respond with another photo, create an accompanying music track, or write a new poem in response to this image spark.

HAIKONOGRAPHY

In Haikonography, students mash together their knowledge of poetry, content, and visualization to craft purpose-driven haiku in icons (page 177). The extent to which students understand poetic devices defines the structural possibilities they might explore.

The degree to which students understand the content establishes the conceptual ideas they might express.

And students' capacity for visualization determines the variety of raw materials they might access.

Similarly, "Playlist a Life" (page 195) calls upon student knowledge of music, tone, and biography. "Five-Course Meal" (page 254) draws out student experience with food, metaphor, and process. And "Chronological Choreography" (page 231) pulls from student familiarity with dance, timeline, and fact.

Critical creativity presents something of a system of checks and balances, ensuring that to achieve the higher-order thinking, students must have approval of all three branches: structural, contextual, and creative.

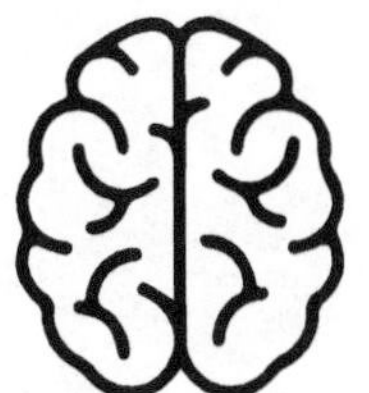

The more students know about a subject, the richer their opportunities to demonstrate that knowledge in a creative medium. And the more practice and exploration with artistic mediums, the more effective the students will be in conveying information and understanding in ways that engage audiences and convey the intended meaning. There is room for both creative expression and content knowledge; the depth of understanding informs the process of creating, and the success of the creation in conveying meaning relies upon truly knowing the content.

If they build it,
they will get it.

IF YOU CAN SEE THINGS OUT OF WHACK THEN YOU CAN SEE HOW THEY CAN BE IN WHACK

THEODOR SEUSS GEISEL

Whimsy

Content

Pathways

Serious Play

Representation

Chutzpah

Empathy

Clarity

Standards

Purpose

WHY

Medium

Analysis

Imagination

CHAPTER 2

CHUTZPAH AND WHIMSY, CONTENT AND CLARITY: TAKING CHANCES ON IMAGINATION

UNPACKING STANDARDS opens new pathways to UNDERSTANDING.

At the intersection of IMAGINATION and INTENTION, we must ask "why?"

Serious play builds CREATIVE CONFIDENCE.

The first few days of any given school year are usually thick with classroom play. Get-to-know-you games and icebreakers abound as students learn the names of classmates and teachers take account of introverts and extroverts, rule-followers, and errant rebels. As the days progress and the curriculum kicks into gear, those moments tend to fall by the wayside. There might be an opportunity here and there to draw a comic strip or illustrate a concept. There might be a free-writing moment here or a sharing circle there, but most often, the next round of play comes as a review session. Kahoot, Socrative, Quizlet and other digital quiz-based tools bring competitive play to bear on learning and fire up students just in time for the next summative test. Then we tuck play back into its box until the next unit is nearly done.

What might happen if whimsy and play were part of the typical, everyday learning in the classroom?

How might a spirit of whimsy affect a student's anxieties about not being a creative person?

How might incorporating play challenge you to design brief, yet meaningful, creative endeavors for your students?

How might you create more opportunities for students to practice creativity and explore in low-stakes, high-yield environments? And what would happen if you did?

How might you then evolve these little explorations into more rigorous applications of knowledge?

UNPACKING STANDARDS OPENS NEW PATHWAYS TO UNDERSTANDING

There's certainly enough controversy and opinion to go around with regards to national, regional, and local curricular standards. Regardless of personal or pedagogical feelings toward mandates or commonalities, aligning classroom instruction and learning to any set of standards is a challenge most educators face. And it is also an opportunity.

When you take the time to unpack standards, flip them upside down, shake them about, and examine their angles and edges, you'll very likely discover opportunities for critical creativity and making meaning through making.

Take, for example, Common Core State Standard ELA.LIT.RL.9–10.7, "Integration of Knowledge and Ideas," which asks ninth- and tenth-grade students to

> "analyze the representation of a subject or key scene in two different artistic mediums, including what is emphasized or absent in each treatment."

The example cited suggests a pairing of W.H. Auden's poem "Musée des Beaux Arts" and Pieter Bruegel's painting of ***Landscape with the Fall of Icarus.***

Without unpacking the standard, it is easy to confuse this example for a demand to compare and contrast Auden and Bruegel. But, if you don't have significant knowledge of modernist British poetry, you might feel anxiety surface when you think about teaching Auden. Similarly, tension may rise when you think about how to teach Bruegel without deep background on Renaissance-era painters from the Netherlands. Is it time to roll out the Venn diagrams and call it good?

Wait. Relax. Don't allow yourself to be distracted by the example.

Instead, take a deeper look at the language of the standard and work to distill its intentions. In doing so, you will find more possibilities for richer experiences than first suggested.

Start with the verbs. What is it students are being asked to do?

Analyze. Break down the art. Take apart the poem. Figure out how the piece does what it does. Ask, ***How does the work achieve the effect it has on the viewer, the reader, or the audience?*** Seek to understand what the piece represents and how its creator establishes that meaning. Determine what artistic medium—the skill, tool, or device—the creator uses to create impact.

REPRESENTATION

Whether in word, image, audio, or object, representations can take many forms. They may be literal or figurative, concrete or abstract. They may move or remain static. They may be obvious or obscure, entertaining or informative. They may be any combination of the above, crossing genres or rocking dynamic.

A representation might come from the subject or key scene. It might be a moment in a narrative, a point of tension, or a space of resolve. It might be a common experience or an object of relative value. It might even be a shared ideal or controversial concept.

ARTISTIC MEDIUM

Painting. Poetry. Drama. Animation. Sculpture. Film. Dance. Puppetry. Song. Pantomime. These and more. Pick two different ones and ask, ***What is emphasized*** or ***absent in each treatment? Treatment*** describes the combination of the subject, the medium, and the representation. It's an artistic technical word that encapsulates the rest of the standard.

And note the "or" in the question above. It may suffice to focus on emphasis: ***What did the creator really want the audience to notice? How was this accomplished?*** It may be okay to focus on absence: ***What did the creator leave out? What did the creator choose not to include in this work that one might expect?*** Emphasis **or** absence, there's no need for students to try to assert something that isn't there or for you to drive yourself batty looking for examples that allow students to assert both.

And there's certainly no requirement here to have students comparing and contrasting the two works, unless that's a cognitive skill one would like to address. Sure, it seems like a natural fit, but that's not being asked for in this standard.

AN EXAMPLE OF INTENTIONAL, CRITICAL CREATIVITY AT WORK

Since poetic devices show up in so many other standards, students often have prior knowledge of these devices without realizing it—oxymorons, personification, repetition, etc. Poetry sits at the core of so many other art forms; it makes both practical and artistic sense to explore it early and often. After all, critical creativity is content agnostic.

There's so much gorgeous verse inspired by history and culture, and so much math and science behind the functionality of poetic devices, that crossing curricula via poetry seems a harmonious fit. Select a handful of poetic terms that feel developmentally appropriate for your students and align well to other curricular goals. You might choose the three above and add metaphor and simile for a group of ninth graders. Bring out some exemplars, brief exercises and experimentations, and formative assessments to check for understanding as you build students' poetry vocabulary.

Returning to the standard in question reveals no requirement that students look at professional works of art. So what if ***students created the works of art to analyze rather than relying upon published, professional pieces***? What if you chose a ***universal experience*** to capture?

For example, *lunch*.

Pose this fairly straight-forward design challenge:

> *"How might we capture what lunchtime means to us individually through a single photograph?"*

The one-page project outline clearly identifies the creative constraints: **one photograph.** The rubric accompanying the assignment could be simply laid out:

- ***subject matter***—It must capture your feelings about lunch to the extent you feel comfortable sharing
- ***composition knowledge***—The photo must make intentional use of emphasis or exclusion (absence) of at least one other composition element learned from a recent photo workshop (i.e., rule of thirds, movement, perspective, etc.)
- ***effective habits of work***—The degree to which the photo has been submitted on time

With clear creative constraints, the students can get to work. They put their composition knowledge to use through handheld devices, cameras from the library's A/V collection, or that they brought from home. They take numerous photos. Many are wonderful. Many are terrible. It is okay. They are experimenting and trying out all sorts of interesting things. They throw those images into a photo editor and play with filters of all sorts. Keep reminding them about ***intentionality***—**play with purpose.**

They choose their best work to submit to peer critique—critique sessions that have a simple rubric asking students to practice ***empathy*** (another habit of work), as they deliver their feedback to use the technical language of photography (key to our standard at play), and to identify moments of emphasis and/or absence in the work (another key component of our standard). Creator intentions are held up to the magnifying glass. Take notes on student observations. Remind the critics to use the technical terms in their critiques, for doing so turns their critiques into an opportunity for formative assessment of their analytical acumen.

Some students may choose to document their critiques of peer photography through the graphic organizer you provide. Others record audio commentary. Others shoot a long-armed selfie video. They are equally relevant because

what matters right now is **quality of analysis,** not the medium through which the evidence is delivered.

By choosing a medium that plays to their strengths, the barrier to communicating understanding is lowered, **the analysis becomes the focus rather than the stress of expressing it**, and as a bonus, you get to experience a little ***variety*** in the assessment process. You might even choose to increase student investment and accountability by inviting students to take part in the process of determining the rubric development and identifying the qualities of a successful product based on their experience. Remember: If they build it, they will get it.

After applying the feedback from the critiques, perhaps taking some new photos altogether, students puts their best works in a Google Drive folder available to the entire class. From that folder, each student then curates an intentional collection of four photos based on one of two criteria—emphasis or absence. They might choose four photos that emphasize a particular idea, four photos that exclude a particular idea, or four photos that emphasize particular ideas ***through*** the absence of a particular idea.

They gather their collection in slideshows and share them on their blogs or perhaps the class website. For added power, print the photos and curate galleries in the cafeteria, hallways, or other common spaces. The curators explain their intentions, and the curated collection serves as evidence that the students can apply their analytical skills across a number of works and demonstrates their understanding of how absence and emphasis work.

And we are . . . not done. We have only provided students the opportunity to partially meet the standard, even if they have created beautiful photography, delivered eloquent critique, and curated intentional collections. Students have tackled one artistic medium, but not yet another.

So we dive into poetry with a substitution to our original design challenge. "How might we capture what lunchtime means to us individually through a poem?"

Students sit in the cafeteria, just as Thoreau floated upon the pond and Whitman sat upon the leaves of grass, composing lines of verse with the criteria in mind. As before, identify the creative constraints:

- ***capture the subject matter***—your feelings about lunch to the extent you feel comfortable sharing
- ***employ poetic devices***—at least two of those we have studied
- ***demonstrate strong habits of work***—revisions and timely drafts

The peer-critique process occurs again, this time the poetry is at the core. An added layer of analytical challenge for the critics—to determine what the pieces emphasize and/or exclude. As photographers, they were expected to be deliberate in those particular choices and make them known. As poets, the intentions may be less self-evident.

After the poems receive feedback and undergo revision, create another Drive folder, start another round of sharing, and establish curated collections. Now the students are editors of online poetry journals, selecting four pieces that again either include or exclude particular subject matter, ideas, or points of view. The illustrations for these journals? The student photography.

The ***intention behind their journal*** is the subject of their final self-assessment, another written or recorded piece that outlines exactly ***what*** their publication intends to tell the reader about lunch, ***why*** each piece was chosen, and the **emphasis or absence evident** in each.

By unpacking this standard,

we have found opportunities for students to be POETS and PHOTOGRAPHERS, to serve as CURATORS and EDITORS, and to publish their work for an authentic audience.

Students have been held accountable for demonstrating the content-area analytical skills called for in the standard, while **making something that matters.** Why choose lunch as the subject? Because lunch is universal in schools—everyone has a designated time to eat—and because that time of day has some form of emotional resonance for most adolescents. Choosing subject matter with an **emotional center** provides added opportunities for empathy, authentic understanding, and to bring relevance to the forefront in our classrooms.

To get there, we need to delve more deeply into the ***why of whimsy.***

AT THE INTERSECTION OF IMAGINATION AND INTENTION, WE MUST ASK "WHY?"

Another expectation exists between the lines: the *why*. The standard in the example above doesn't require students to speculate upon the creator's intentions, simply to break it down: analyze it, unravel it, deconstruct it, and/or reverse engineer it. Some people may argue that it is impossible to know an artist's true intentions and that assessing a student's ability to do so is either a fool's errand, unfair, or both. However, exploring those intentions is precisely the sort of thinking students need to do in order to bring value to the entire analytical process.

When students learn how something works, they can then ***apply that knowledge to another context***—another time, place, and circumstance. Exploring the why and attempting to understand intention increases the likelihood of transferring that analysis to other contexts, especially those most unlike the original. Will most students need to apply rhyming couplet to a poem later in life? Not likely. Will most students see a need to apply a rhythmic pattern to delivering an emotional speech or composing a persuasive e-mail? Experience suggests yes. Taking time to hypothesize on a creator's intentions based on available evidence and rigorous analysis pushes student thinking that much higher up Bloom's taxonomy and that much further along any Depth of Knowledge scale.

In making a case for *why*, students become active agents in the work, empathizing with the creator, seeing the problem the creator sees, and understanding why this particular solution seems appropriate. Perhaps students find themselves as critics of those solutions, seeing other strategies and tactics they believe may better serve the creator. They build their own repertoire to address the challenges surfacing in their own lives. Students only arrive here by first identifying and then analyzing the function of the creator's tools—meeting the call of the standard—and then delving into the intentionality evident. These are the spaces where the authentic value of academic skills and knowledge make themselves known, if we pause long enough to recognize them.

The degree of intention tends to correlate to the degree of understanding. For example, in a few moments, almost all students can create a color palette on ColourLovers.com.

They can then label those colors with superficial names that vaguely relate to a given concept, say, the anatomy of a cell. But it takes a student who truly understands the functionality of each organelle to rename an electric blue, "mitochondriatic blue," and explain that her choice stems from knowing mitochondria are the powerhouses of the cell and that her choice to rename that soft gray, "semipermeable membrane," is because a little light is coming through the dark, just like some materials pass through a cell's coating.

And it takes an educator who is aware of which skills and knowledge are being assessed to allow students to write, record, sketchnote, film, present, or otherwise convey their intentions in **whatever medium best enables that student's explanation**. Of course,

as you hold students accountable for sharing their creative reasoning, you are giving them an opportunity to develop their writing, speaking, and/or visual media skills.

Why do creative-critical thinking and meaningful making play so nicely with standards-based learning? Assessment systems that allow a single product to serve as evidence for a number of standards, say reading comprehension, writing composition, and vocabulary, become powerful platforms for integrating creativity into the classroom because educators can easily distinguish student achievement from one criterion to the next. Thus, a student might create an aesthetically gorgeous painting of a 1960s civil-rights protest march and put it up for the teacher to critique in a one-on-one conference.

"Mike, that's a fantastic-looking painting. Could you tell me about it?"

"Sure. It's uh . . . it's a watercolor of the march in Selma."

"Cool. I am loving your use of color in the sky and how it contrasts with the colors used in the marchers. What was your thinking there?"

"Uh . . . well . . . I ran out of red and yellow, so I had to do the sky in blue."

"Okay, and what was your thinking behind the faces?"

"What about them?"

"You didn't include any facial features, like, at all. Was that intentional or . . . ?"

"I'm not good at faces."

"Gotcha. What would you like me to notice?"

"It took me, seriously, forever to do this."

"I can tell. Do you have your write-up?"

"I emailed it to you."

"So you did. Lemme take a look . . . ah . . . question for you. When was the march on Selma?"

"In the sixties . . ."

"Right, that was a big decade, though. Ten years, in fact. It's important that you have a sense of chronology and sequence."

"1968."

"It was actually 1965. How about you take another look at your write-up and review those articles and graphic novel excerpts we used the other day? Look specifically at the Civil Rights Act because I wanted you folks to work the language of the act into either the art or your explanation. Bring a new draft on Thursday, and we can talk about what you might do with your painting to amp up its intentionality. I got a feeling we might be able make those colors mean something more than just what you had available. And the faces, too, might be a happy accident."

The painting easily meets a visual-media standard, but when sharing his intentions, Mike reveals lack of factual understanding regarding the movement. Further, he fails to use the content-specific vocabulary accurately in his presentation. Questions asked about his intentions behind the painting reveal only a surface level of understanding, with no meaning given to the anonymous faces or color scheme. If the teacher were to put Mike's achievement in a classic grade sausage-grinder, he might end up with anything from a B to a D. However, by employing best practices of standards-based assessment, it's possible to distinguish the creative achievement from the critical thinking and content achievement and present a much more accurate story of student knowledge. Mike met the standard for visual media, but he did not meet his vocabulary standard and only partially met the reading comprehension standards. Provided opportunity for revision along with some guidance and actionable feedback, Mike may be able to better put his artistic skills to academic work.

Meaningful making is largely contingent on students' **capacity for creative reasoning** and a teacher's willingness to allow students **multiple means for sharing the lineage** of that project. In the **explanation of intent**, a student's seemingly unsuccessful product—a raggedy collage, a poem blistered with misspellings, a nine-minute YouTube opus consisting primarily of outtakes—may actually prove its value.

SERIOUS PLAY BUILDS CREATIVE CONFIDENCE

As mentioned before, Albert Einstein believed that **"combinatorial play"**—the mashing up of ideas, seeing relationships where others don't—is the basis for all productive thought. The notion of "play" is important, because creativity often stems from ***whimsy, tinkering, and humor.*** In fact, **David Ogilvy**, one of the original "Mad Men" of the mid-century advertising world, believed the best ideas start as jokes. Because play is ***a way*** of approaching thought and learning, there is no need for it to be a time-consuming addition to an already strapped-for-time course. Creative thinking and making exercises can be used for any age level and in any discipline. As comedian and writer John Cleese says,

"Creativity is not a talent. It is a way of operating."

Although humans have been making a creative mark on the world since those first handprints in the caves, it must be noted that a major paradigm shift in the creative landscape has occurred, especially since the late twentieth century. It's called **participatory culture**, and, as the guru of this field, media scholar Henry Jenkins reminds us, we now ***"live in a world in which everyone has access to the means of creative expression and the networks supporting artistic distribution."***

This access is the ultimate game changer. Easy-to-use tools (particularly digital tools and platforms) have allowed the average person to become a published author, musician, actor, photographer, and artist. As media theorist Marshall McLuhan insisted, ***"We shape our tools, and then our tools shape us."***

But creativity plays an even more important role than in the arts and literature—it is only through the ability to **think creatively** that we can begin to tackle the challenges in an unpredictable future world. The rate of change has proven to be exponential—there is no way to foresee what kind of work we will be doing in the years to come, and how we will need to do it. A major responsibility of education is to **cultivate creative thinkers and makers**.

Students need to be asked to do more than remember, regurgitate, rehash, and reiterate. Active making coupled with daily creative-thinking strategies help students learn to: observe and interpret, find patterns and draw analogies, evaluate and question, and explore varying perspectives. They become **critical consumers** who effectively search, wisely critique, purposefully curate, and thoughtfully annotate what they find on the web. Curation is akin to creativity in that it is about *collecting* dots, finding relationships, providing context, and articulating and sharing the significance. And students become meaningful makers in their own right, leveraging both analog and digital tools in order to express their understandings and feelings about a particular subject or add new context—to be involved in ***knowledge production*** themselves.

What gives something learned

poignancy

(a word that comes from the Latin word "***to prick***")?

If students find an emotional connection or a direct relevance to their lives, they are more likely to internalize the knowledge.

With an interdisciplinary, thematic approach, students can ***think about connections:*** within the course, to other courses, and to life (aka "the real world"). They can learn about grand ideas, not items.

In doing creative projects that involve designing and making, students also practice ***perseverance, collaboration, and problem solving*** while they refine their ***focus and confidence.***

Overcoming self-doubt in order to develop **creative courage** is perhaps the most difficult hurdle. We (students, teachers, all humans who want to exercise creativity) must be free from the vise (or vice!) of self-doubt and learn to tune out the internal editor that tells us we are not good enough. The most important thing you can do to help students with this process is to foster a culture and community of **care and respect**. If care and respect comprise the underlying tone of your class, topped with a sense of light-heartedness, students will feel free to take creative risks. It doesn't hurt to show your own work as well. Think about including personal creative projects such as photography, painting, or poetry in your classroom (after all, it is a teacher's second home). Share stories of performing improv at an out-of-town club and the challenges of rehearsing for a gig. Show the music parody videos you made with your friends and discuss the behind-the-scenes technical process. Be transparent in your thinking by writing your creative checklist on the wall behind your desk. What are you working on? What do you hope to accomplish? Sharing your works-in-progress demonstrates to students you are a co-learner (an excellent term used by Howard Rheingold), a thinker, and a creator in your own right.

Sometimes a mere change in labels can influence the ways in which we think about ourselves. In what ways might you use **self-talk** or **imagination** to think of yourself in a different way in order to spur creativity? How could you empower your students to find new and more beneficial ways in which to think about themselves? In a fascinating experiment with the **"stereotype effect,"** researchers claimed that people who imagined themselves to be **"an eccentric poet"** rather than a "rigid librarian" scored better on creativity tests in both fluency and originality.

Amy pulled a Mary Poppins "spoonful of sugar" euphemism with her classes. She developed a metaphor called **the Café, the Studio, and the Stage.** The most surprising thing she noticed was that when she started calling "work time" ***"studio time,"*** students' attitudes shifted. The same effect happens with switching "groups" to ***"design teams."*** Thinking of the classroom as a studio and your students as artists make all the difference. *Studio time* is the "white space" for executing a project. During this time, students can plan, work together, build, and create. Teachers may walk around the room and help students troubleshoot, guide their direction, and encourage them to refine their work. What if you assign a **class "paparazzo"** to archive the process by taking photos? Finally, think like a designer: Talk about "***specs***" rather than "criteria," and provide a ***"design brief"*** rather than an *"assignment."*

David Kelley, founder of global design firm IDEO and creator of the Stanford d.School, and his brother, Tom, an IDEO partner in his own right, coined the term "creative confidence" to describe a person's belief in his or her ability to make change

FAIL FLAMBOYANTLY
MALCOLM MCLAREN

happen—to address needs, to develop solutions, to innovate the status quo, to create something needed, wanted, and necessary. Creative confidence is organic—it comes from within and grows with experience. It requires exercise to thrive, lest it atrophy and beleaguer the maker.

Classrooms have potential to be the greatest gyms in the world for students to work on their creative confidence. Move the muscle groups around. Do some work on the visuals. Then let those rest while some kinesthetic movement gets the spatial reasoning going as well. Get a drink, and then play some pickup games with music and do a few laps around the fabricating track. Cool down with a critique and hydrate. Tomorrow, change it up. Create confusion. Amplify the growth. Make a plan. Stick to it while it works, and then modify as needed.

It makes sense that we don't slow down enough for this work. There seems to be a constant expectation for educators to do more with less and to do so with peak efficiency. Pressure for coverage over depth is applied daily by policymakers who are concerned with data and media cycles and use headlines as their chief currency.

If we want to help students succeed not only in school but also in *life*, we must make time for play. Students will fare better on standardized tests as experienced critical thinkers—after all, most tests are more puzzles to be solved than authentic demonstrations of content knowledge. And the skill of critical thinking is much more desirous to higher-learning institutions and employers than the ability to simply regurgitate information.

Aligning creative classroom experiences to curricular goals heightens the creative confidence factor as well, particularly when coupled with authentic problem solving and genuine audiences. Students seeing others enjoying their art, films, songs, and podcasts gain a deeper appreciation for their own abilities. Students who witness their newfound knowledge addressing a need and making life better for someone or something gain yet another degree of resolve. This is true innovation—a creative endeavor adding value to society.

So, unpack the standards. Take notes. Doodle. Sketch. Outline. List. Explore the standard in a way that makes sense to you. And then repeat the process with your students. Ask questions about what the terms mean. Collaborate on paraphrasing that aligns to the spirit of the standard. Risk vulnerability. Share the work you did on your own and cast it in the light of student insights. Share your collective ideas with colleagues both near and far. Get their input. See how their takes may inform yours. Look for alignments and congruences and seek out inspiration in the outliers and in interpretations that challenge conventional wisdom.

Do this often enough—by yourself, with students, with colleagues, with your personal/professional learning network—and the growing familiarity will reveal those ***eureka*** moments that ignite powerful learning. Additionally, that familiarity will lead to more effortless recall, providing more space and energy for the unexpected to bubble up and for the serendipitous collision of whimsy and content to spark a shower of powerful learning and inspire creativity. And if there's one thing we love, it is serendipity.

IT'S LOOKING AT THINGS FOR A LONG TIME THAT RIPENS YOU AND GIVES YOU A DEEPER MEANING

VINCENT VAN GOGH

Rose Bud Thorn

Rigorous Whimsy

Authenticity

TO WHAT EXTENT

Proposal Audience

Process

Assessment

NO DUMPSTER PROJECTS

Pondering

Feedback

Notice Wish Wonder

CHAPTER 3

NO MORE DUMPSTER PROJECTS: TRANSFORMING FLIGHTS OF FANCY INTO PATHWAYS TO AUTHENTICITY

Assess the CONTENT, not the CREATIVITY.

WELL-CRAFTED FEEDBACK delineates the content from the form and the process from the product.

Audience breeds AUTHENTICITY, heightens INTENTION, and promotes PURPOSE.

Purging the classroom of student projects can be one of the most anxious, unsettling, and altogether unpleasant experiences of the entire school year. It also requires a deft hand, a calloused heart, and impeccable timing. One must know how to fold and bend cardboard and poster paper in upon itself, obscuring identifiable markings as it goes into those far-too-thin plastic bags. One must not waver or raise the question, "Should I keep it or should it go?" for such weakness leads to closets bursting with soon-forgotten mobiles and shadowboxes. And one must know the custodians' routines, minimizing the likelihood that creators of those discarded game boards and trifolds stumble upon their work as it waits to be hauled away to the Landfill of Forgotten Assignments. (No one wants a Popsicle-stick model of the Lincoln Memorial or a squirt gun that shoots strawberry jam.)

However, these stresses are largely avoidable, starting with the adoption of a simple mantra:

no dumpster projects.

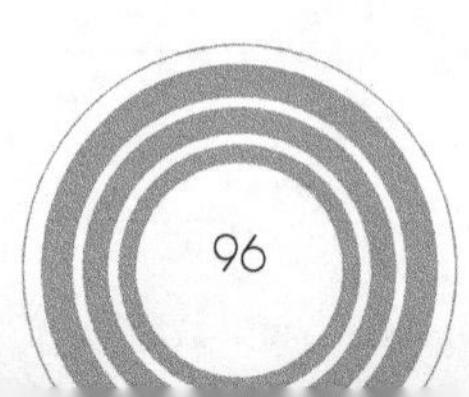

GMS
01773 541 372

What if you repeated that mantra every time you design a summative assessment? Each time you craft criteria for capstone events? Each time you distribute rubrics to students? ***No more dumpster projects***. How might such an approach challenge you to be more ***intentional with your assessments*** and engage students in more authentic demonstrations of understanding? And how might such a mindset enable you to expand your flights of whimsy and playfulness into powerful evidence of learning?

No more dumpster projects.

Transforming quick and exploratory formative assessments into more robust and rigorous summative assessments doesn't have to be a stressful or square-peg-into-round-hole experience. In fact, doing so allows students to **see every learning experience in the classroom as having equal merit and value.** And at the same time, you will force yourself to be that much more thoughtful about each lesson's place in the bigger picture.

ASSESS THE CONTENT, NOT THE CREATIVITY

"I'm just not a creative person, so I don't feel comfortable assigning creative assignments."

"How do I know if a student's sculpture is good or not? I'm not a sculptor."

"All of those things made of LEGOs look really neat and all, but how do you grade something like that?"

We field questions like these on a regular basis. They revolve the common misconception that you have to be a creative in order to assess a student's creative product.

The point is not to assess creativity. The point is to

use creativity as a tool for students to demonstrate what they know.

Far too often, creativity gets relegated to the bottom of the junk drawer where empty packing-tape dispensers and Allen wrenches hide until they are needed. Instead, creativity should be right there on the countertop beside the whisks, spatulas, and that gorgeous set of knives your spouse bought you last year because nothing compares to a well-balanced blade when it comes to slicing vegetables. The more you apply creativity to learning experiences of all sorts, the more comfortable you will become with not just designing those experiences but also with the artful task of separating the content from the form and assessing what really matters: ***the depth of student understanding.***

Comic-book creator Scott McCloud explores the concept of separating content from form in his seminal work, ***Understanding Comics.*** In trying to define what makes comics comics, McCloud argues people tend to mix the content—the plots, the characters, the themes—together with the form—the panel sequencing, the art, the lettering. As such, one gets mistaken for the other. Lumping the content and form together muddies the waters and leads to misunderstandings that spandex-clad superheroes and hijinks-prone kids from Riverdale are essential qualities to comics. The reality is that comics are an agile and complex art form that McCloud and comic-book luminary Will Eisner define as "sequential art," a term that can be boiled down ***to related images placed in a particular order to produce a desired narrative effect***.

Steven Johnson takes McCloud's thinking and applies it across the pop-culture landscape in his book ***Everything Bad Is Good For You***. Comics, movies, television, and video games all possess a richness. The very best of each of these media categories challenges our cognition and forces us to think. Unfortunately, critics get caught up in the content, pointing to violent video games and choreographed reality television as evidence of a lack in value. Johnson and McCloud urge us to push the content away for a moment and examine the complexities inherent to each form and the possibilities each affords.

Do the opposite.

Sculpture, puppetry, ballet, stop-motion, pastels, kisekae, beatbox—each of these art forms has distinguishable qualities, as well as best practices and standards for excellence in the craft. When assessing a student's product borne of critical creativity, put all of that to the side and **focus only on the content.**

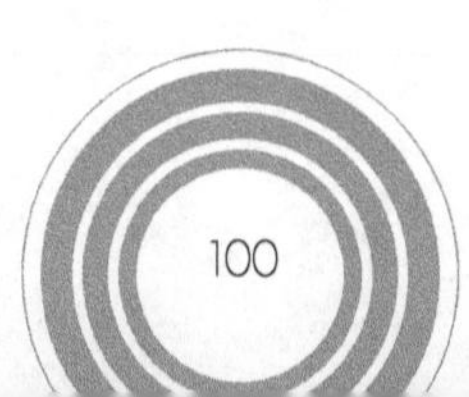

Ask . . .
To what extent

...are the ideas presented factual, accurate, and/or based upon evidence?

...have the targeted understandings been presented—fully, partially, or not quite yet?

...have the key concepts been applied to a relevant and/or new context?

...have the content area skills been demonstrated?

...have the essential questions been answered and/or reframed?

...have the user's needs been met and/or problem been solved?

These are questions educators should be asking of student work no matter what assessment format, be it a quiz, test, essay, sonnet, five-course meal, or mobile app.

Focus on the learning that is evident in the product. When you step back from the painting or put the film on pause, when the mobile stops turning and the cursor goes back to the top of the screen, what is there? What does this student appear to know and be able to do? Where does this student seem to be missing the core concept or being misled in understanding? Yes, it is beautiful. Yes, it is impressive. Yes, it causes smiles or laughter and may even make you want to share it on social media. Yes, you might even want to buy it and put it on your living room wall. That's all wonderful. But the real question is, ***does it do the thing it absolutely needs to do in order to serve as evidence of deep, rich, authentic understanding?***

This is rigorous whimsy.

WELL-CRAFTED FEEDBACK DELINEATES THE CONTENT FROM THE FORM AND THE PROCESS FROM THE PRODUCT

Student knowledge grows most effectively when learning experiences are coupled with feedback. Feedback is fuel for continued creativity. While creating for creation's sake has its place, when looking for students to demonstrate deep, critical thinking and higher-order problem-solving skills, they need feedback to validate their experiences and ***activate the next stages*** in their understanding.

Feedback should be specific and constructive. It should raise questions and foster deeper thinking. Platitudes like "Great!" and "Wonderful!" have their place, but those exclamations must be accompanied by reasoning. After all, if we are going to hold students accountable for their intentions, shouldn't we hold ourselves to similar standards?

In addition to the expected feedback from you, students should be given an opportunity to respond to others' work and to share their feelings about their own work. Providing feedback to another validates a student's place in the classroom as an equal and as a co-collaborator. (Moreover, the quality of that feedback can provide useful formative assessment and reveal the extent to which the critic is achieving the curricular goal as well.) In addition to exposing a student's degree of self-worth and confidence, self-assessment may well cause you to notice a feature or intention in the work that you may have otherwise overlooked.

A useful peer-feedback technique developed by Amy is **"Love the . . . What If?"** Say one thing you love about your classmate's work and provide a suggestion for how it could be even better. This places students' minds in the realm of positive possibilities rather than the abyss of negative nitpicking.

A good strategy for self-critique and reflection is what we call affective data gathering. Focus on ***feeling***. Ask students to use an **emoji as an exit ticket** or **create hashtags** to contextualize how they felt about a certain project.

Reflection of the process, a sort of **"show your work,"** is perhaps the most valuable assessment task. Ask students to discuss (not necessarily "write about" because often a video blog is a better way for them to share) their creative influence, inspiration, their design process, tools, and troubleshooting experiences. The latter is really helpful for future students or projects. If you have examples of work from previous students or even professionals, show it—critique of exemplars is one of the most effective ways to get the best work from your students. Encourage them to be thorough and thoughtful.

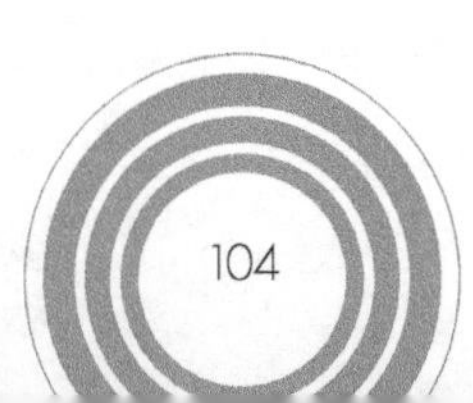

Think of the **three Ps of projects**:

- ***Proposals***
- ***Process***
- ***Pondering (reflection)***

Digitizing exemplars is your best bet because they can be easily stored and recalled for future use. If students have blog portfolios, ask them to post every piece of work and the contextualization of that work on their blogs, and post the URLs to that work on a shared spreadsheet or document. If they create film projects, have them create a YouTube playlist. Pin down Twitter chats with a tool such as Storify.com. Create a class wiki, website, or Google+ community to post tagged (therefore, searchable) photographs of student work and students in the process of working. Consider assigning a "class paparazzi" team as mentioned in the previous chapter.

Exemplars are undeniably the most effective tool in maximizing the quality of student work. Critiquing former student work (the good, the "meh," and the ugly) gives current students perspective—they know what is possible, what has been done before, and what they might do to make something even better. It's helpful to be a curator of professional content as well (or, ask students to help with this). For example, before tackling stop-motion animation, Amy's students looked at a variety of styles from across the web, including famous Viners and Instagrammers.

While most educators must operate within the confines of a task-specific rubric, consider applying some sort of "universal specs" to creative work. If the immediate goal is to ***demonstrate knowledge and understanding,*** and the ultimate goal is to ***leave a legacy,*** you could propose the following:

It is easy to become distracted by the vehicle by which students convey their understanding. Misspelled text and thick puddles of white-out, awkward video edits, and garish color schemes can all pull attention away from assessing whether or not the students know what we want them to know. Applying more deliberate and intentional tools and protocols helps everyone, teachers and students, provide more useful feedback.

Design tools like "Notice, Wish, Wonder" and "Rose, Bud, Thorn" are flexible feedback protocols that can be applied at any stage in the creation process.

I noticed the pace of the video edits increased as the action in the storyline picked up.

I noticed the font was difficult to read when it was up on the screen.

I noticed facts about Claudette Colvin's life all the way through the film.

I wish I knew how to keep the camera as still as it is during the first-person point-of-view scene.

I wish the film helped explain why Claudette Colvin didn't get as much attention as Rosa Parks.

I wish the music seemed as intentional as the rest of the film.

I wonder what would happen if you asked a friend to perform a song for the soundtrack on this film.

I wonder why you chose that font for the title screen.

I wonder if the film might be a minute shorter because it seemed like some of the takes were quite long.

Once students use the **Notice-Wish-Wonder approach** to provide feedback a number of times, those stems become part of the learning culture and a regular part of the students' vocabulary. The same is true for the **Rose-Bud-Thorn approach**. Rather than stems, however, these are categories of feedback. Roses are positives that stand out, thorns are negatives that ought to be addressed, and buds are opportunities to grow and expand on what is present.

Roses might include the use of edits and transitions, the consistent use of factual information, and the steady camera work.

Thorns might include the font that is difficult to read and the music that seemed unintentional.

Buds might be enlisting a peer to create music for the film, the longer takes that might be edited down, and the opportunity to expand more comparisons between Claudette Colvin and Rosa Parks.

Many schools require teachers to use rubrics to provide students clear expectations and assist in the learning process. Once controversial, they are now nearly ubiquitous with more schools familiar with grids of criteria than not. That does not mean they are any easier to design or any more effective. Rubrics can be fantastic tools for gauging student achievement or mind-numbing exercises in futility. They may guide and constrain just as easily they might prescribe and constrict. It is all about how they are designed and implemented. There are two different tactics for rubric design that prove useful in the pursuit of assessing critical creativity.

The first is the traditional four-point scale rubric, easily adaptable to any model of curriculum and assessment that may be present in your impact area.

	Pet Sounds	Nevermind	Kingdom Come	Uncle Morty's Jugband Jamboree
Playlist Explanations To what extent have you composed effective rationales (one paragraph each) explaining each of your tracks? How clear is it why they are included? How much detail have you included? (WRITING)	I love how you include three or more effective, detailed rationales that explain the reasons why those songs are on the playlist in a unique, interesting or insightful way.	I like how you included three effective, detailed rationales that explain the reason why those songs are on the playlist.	I noticed you only have two effective rationales. How might I help you better prove your thinking? How else might you show why this song is so perfect for the playlist?	What's up? I notice you don't have many rationales here or the ones you have aren't really doing the job yet. How can I help?
Evidence of Empathy To what extent have you demonstrated an understanding of another's point of view and needs? (HABITS of MIND)	I love how your rationales and finished product reveal an exceptional, insightful understanding of your user's needs.	I like how your rationales and finished product reveal a solid understanding of your user's needs.	I noticed your product and your rationales don't seem to show much understanding of your user's needs; how might you gather more understanding of who they are and what they need?	What's up? I'm not seeing any evidence at all that you've thought about someone else's needs here. How can I help?
Complete Playlist How well designed is your playlist cover art and the covers for each side? Tracklisting? Compile the actual music? (MEDIA)	I love how your final product completely takes on the shape, form, and function of a playlist with professional-looking album art that shows unique, interesting or clever use of design skills. I can listen to it!	I like how your final product takes on the shape, form, and function of a soundtrack with effective album art for each side that shows basic design skills.	I noticed your final product seems unfinished or rushed when I look at it; how might you get inspiration for the cover art from other covers? How might you collect your music?	What's up? I didn't see any cover art or what I did . . . well . . . it doesn't seem like a finished product at all. Also, where's the music? How can I help?

	Pet Sounds	Nevermind	Kingdom Come	Uncle Morty's Jugband Jamboree
Sources & Citations Where are the sources for these ideas? Has credit been given to images, sounds, etc.? (RESEARCH)	I love how clear it is to me you used an effective resource to exceed this standard; 100 percent MLA format accuracy in works cited of all words, images, sounds, and ideas presented.	I like that your works cited seems pretty darn error free except for those ornery moments that most folks wouldn't notice.	I'm concerned by the number of errors I'm seeing here. What resources could you use to better cite sources and create a works cited page?	What's up? I know MLA format is hard to memorize, which is why I tell folks to just know where you can look it up fast. Your errors here are distracting from your bigger point. How can I help?
Professional Quality Spelling, mechanics, formatting, appearance, crispness (MUGS)	I love how rich and powerful your use of language is. You clearly have command of your mechanics et al. and use them in the service of your style.	I like how well you use your language. When I notice errors, they do not interfere at all. How might you improve your MUGS so that you may develop a stronger personal style?	I'm concerned with how many errors showed up in your language. (I may also be concerned that your writing was too short to be assessed this way.) What tools/ resources could help you with proofreading and editing?	What's up? It seems like you failed to proofread at all. How might I help you get your MUGS on track?
Thinking and Creating Process To what extent have you documented your process? #showyourwork (HABITS of MIND)	I love how varied, plentiful, and useful the evidence demonstrating the process of your thinking and product development appears to be.	I like the evidence I'm seeing that demonstrates the process of your thinking and product development for this piece.	I notice I'm underwhelmed by the evidence you have provided. What else could you include to show your thinking process and development?	What's up? Why does it seem to be challenging to track your progress? What can I do to make it a little easier?
Timeliness How on time did you submit your work? (ACADEMIC INITIATIVE)	I love that you turned it in on time or even early or by the agreed-upon due date. Boomshakala.	I like that you turned it in before it was a full day late. It happens. Life goes on.	I noticed you turned this in up to 1 week late. How can I help? What might you do to prevent this from happening next time?	What's up? I noticed you turned this in over a week late. How can I help?

Each row features a different criterion, and each criterion aligns to a particular standard. Rubrics might focus on a single standard or several, depending largely on the intention of the learning experience, the time budgeted for the experience, and the degree to which students will have the opportunity to revise their learning. Layering in several standards can ensure a rich experience and help students make the cognitive connections between form, function, and content. Be careful, however; too many layers can grow unwieldy, not just for the students but also for you as the educator. All criteria should receive feedback, and when there are seven aspects of a product to consider, you may run out of time to properly assess the project.

Jennifer Gonzalez, via her blog ***Cult of Pedagogy,*** suggests another approach to rubric design: the single-score point rubric. Rather than parsing out language for each score point along the continuum (a cumbersome task for even the most wizened classroom educator), Gonzalez recommends describing what meeting the expectation looks like for each criterion. To the left and right of that description, provide space for feedback regarding the ways in which the student did not yet meet that goal and ways in which the student exceeded it. The continuum provides more detailed feedback, and the single-score approach speeds up the feedback process. That means less time is spent hemming and hawing back and forth as to which language on the rubric best describes the student's work, and more time can be devoted to providing insights.

When designing a rubric, list the most essential content standard at the top to create a visual hierarchy for students. Also, note separate criteria for the documentation of intention. Student demonstration of intention is vital—that's where you know your students are "getting it." However, you need not assess how well the student expresses that intention unless you want to add that layer.

For example, when Dan asks his students to pitch soundtracks for a production of ***Macbeth***, they must present their choices to the class because he is also assessing their speaking skills. Thus, the presentation receives a separate criterion row on the rubric. The content of that presentation and the students' intentions behind each song reveal the depth of their understanding and becomes essential evidence for assessing their reading comprehension. Frequently, students will meet the criterion for reading comprehension, while only partially meeting the speaking standard, having used notes too frequently and failed to make eye contact, while still delivering content that demonstrates clear understanding of the play, its characters, and the themes. Sometimes, students will possess outstanding presentation skills, virtually selling oceanfront property in Oklahoma via their charisma, but like that shady real-estate deal, the content understanding is notoriously absent.

When intention, creativity, and content intersect, we often find students delivering presentations that exceed the standards. The close reading and semantic connections between lyric, sound, and dramatic verse fuel confidence in their understanding. That confidence then translates over into their pitches and there it is once again—**edusymbiosis:** creativity informing content, informing creativity, and collectively demonstrating deeper understanding.

Single Point Rubric

Criteria	Evidence of Exceeding the Standard (clever, insightful, unique, powerful, creative, meaningful, professional)	What Meeting the Standard Looks Like	Evidence of Needs for Improvement (gaps, missing pieces or evidence, incomplete thoughts)
Playlist Explanations To what extent have you composed effective rationales (one paragraph each) explaining each of your tracks? How clear is it why they are included? How much detail have you included? (WRITING)		I like how you included three effective, detailed rationales that explain the reason why those songs are on the playlist. I like how those details show rather than tell and seem confident that they are accurate.	
Evidence of Empathy To what extent have you demonstrated an understanding of another's point of view and needs? (HABITS of MIND)		I like how your rationales and finished product reveal a solid understanding of your user's needs. I feel like I know who this person is and what they need.	
Complete Playlist How well designed is your playlist cover art and the covers for each side? Tracklisting? Compile the actual music?(MEDIA)		I like how your final product takes on the shape, form, and function of a soundtrack with effective album art for each side that shows basic design skills. I like how the album art feels professional and well considered (font, image, alignment, rule of thirds, etc.)	

Criteria	Evidence of Exceeding the Standard (clever, insightful, unique, powerful, creative, meaningful, professional)	What Meeting the Standard Looks Like	Evidence of Needs for Improvement (gaps, missing pieces or evidence, incomplete thoughts)
Sources & Citations Where are the sources for these ideas? Has credit been given to images, sounds, etc.? (RESEARCH)		I like that your works cited seems pretty darn error free except for those ornery moments that most folks wouldn't notice.	
Professional Quality Spelling, mechanics, formatting, appearance, crispness (MUGS)		I like how well you use your language. When I notice errors, they do not interfere at all. How might you improve your MUGS so that you may develop a stronger personal style?	
Thinking and Creating Process To what extent have you documented your process? #showyourwork (HABITS of MIND)		I like the evidence I'm seeing that demonstrates the process of your thinking and product development for this piece.	

Blogs. Journals. Portfolios. Choose a form of curated collection that works for you. Determine the criteria for entries into that collection. Thus, a student might document any critical-creativity experience in the classroom and place it in the collection to be assessed based on the criteria for that collection.

For formative assessment criteria, develop a generic set of standards that you can apply to any experience in the classroom. This gives you a framework that can be adapted into a summative assessment.

Please do not mistake this focus on content for dismissal of growing one's artistic prowess. We want students exploring all of these forms. We want them diving into how hand-drawn animation works, learning the nuanced differences between a reel and a jig, growing versed in the language of tap, and coating their hands in plaster of Paris. **Art for art's sake is an inherently noble pursuit; it grabs hold of our humanity in a way little else can.** Anything that is art holds emotion, and emotion is more sticky. It lasts. It persists. Thus, the more capacity students have for various art forms, the more avenues present themselves for expressing and retaining content knowledge.

AUDIENCE BREEDS AUTHENTICITY, HEIGHTENS INTENTION, AND PROMOTES PURPOSE

How might educators give students the opportunity to cultivate a network, build a positive presence beyond the classroom walls, and perhaps make something that is part of a legacy? As pop-art guru Andy Warhol described:

> ***"The idea is not to live forever—it is to create something that will."***

Perhaps the most authentic assessment comes from publicly sharing work. It is ideal if students have YouTube channels, their own blog, and a Twitter or Google+ account, but that is sometimes not possible or desirable, depending on the age of students and the district. You can always maintain these as a teacher, but that does not really help students build up a positive digital presence in their name. Blogger **Seth Godin** says: ***"You are not your résumé—you are your work."*** Author of ***Show Your Work*, Austin Kleon,** goes so far as to assert that, ***"If your work isn't online, it doesn't exist."***

To stand out with college-selection boards or as job finalists, students need to have more than good grades. They need a positive digital presence. That presence, cultivated over time—with all the work they put out there—will in essence become their CV (or transcript, if the point is to get you into college). It must be noted we use the term "digital presence" because the commonly used "footprint" is far too past tense and the term "digital tattoo" has negative connotations in addition to being something more passive (a tattoo happens to you) rather than active (you create how you want to be seen on the Internet over time through your work).

When future bosses or college-entrance folks do a Google search for your students, what will they find? You can help make sure they find the good stuff—the academic and artistic goodies—by featuring assignments with students' **real names** online. (Yes, we teach high school, not kindergarten, and there is a difference, but the practice of sharing in more protected ways can start early.) The ability to own one's ideas and work in public speaks to the importance of teaching and fostering digital citizenship early, engaging such resources as Marialice B.F.X. Curran's DigCit Summits and Common Sense Media's vast toolboxes.

We know from experience that online identity ownership works. Amy recalls one girl who came up to her as a high-school senior and said she was pleased that when she did a Google search on herself, her (very thoughtful) blog and film projects from ninth-grade history popped up and not the sketchy party photos from Facebook. One of Dan's recent students was able to land freelance digital marketing gigs by using his real name for a videography passion project he created for class. Other students returned from college and let us know that, although it often seemed overwhelming at the time, learning to manage a variety of social media accounts, produce creative work, and distribute it across channels proved quite helpful to them.

The best way to help students is to **provide them with opportunities to create and share their work.** You perhaps will need to set up an infrastructure to do this. (For example, Amy helped students create their blog sites. She listed a blogroll on her course blog so students could all easily see one another's sites.)

Help students navigate different social media spaces and use social media in the context of the curriculum. Show them how to **amplify their work by sharing it.** Teach them to share their work, and be an advocate by sharing their work with ***your*** social networks. To do this, you will—no surprise here—have to be a connected educator yourself. If you don't have a lot of followers, make sure you know which hashtags to use so that the appropriate audience can find the work. While you're at it, teach students how to leverage hashtags, too. You can start by

using the #FF (Follow Friday) tag to encourage others to follow a student's blog, video channel, Instagram, digital art portfolio, or website.

YOU HAVE TO START SOMEWHERE

It's not easy to transition from a completion-oriented classroom—one dominated by the notion that "anything is better than a zero"—to an intention-driven environment characterized by the credo "no dumpster projects." But if you're reading this, you've already moved further along the mindset continuum toward the belief that purpose comes before grade books.

The rest of this book comprises a catalog of experiences we believe serve as ideal entry points for educators looking to leverage creativity as a means of engaging students in more meaningful demonstrations of learning. You'll find suggestions for applying strategies across content areas. If you're already a deep practitioner of creativity in your classroom, you can use the following ideas as a framework to extend your strategies to even higher-order thinking and more authentic audiences.

Still, every journey starts with the proverbial first step ... the next page is yours.

LEARN
THE
RULES
LIKE
A PRO
SO YOU
CAN BREAK
THEM
LIKE
AN ARTIST
PABLO
PICASSO

CATALOG OF CRITICAL CREATIVITY:

GLOSSARY OF INTENTION ICONS

Suggests elevating catalog entries into deeper learning experiences for students.

Ways to apply each catalog entry to content area learning

Catalog entries focused on kinesthetic critical-creativity experiences

Experience involves photography

Each clock represents 15 minutes

Experience involves computers whether for creation, research, or collaboration

Catalog entries with ELA applications

Experience involves food

Catalog entries with healthy and physical education applications

Catalog entries focused on visual critical-creativity experiences

Experience involves index cards

Experience involves Internet access

Experience involves building bricks

Experience involves doodling, coloring, or labeling

Catalog entries with a mathematics integration focus

Suggests one possible approach to crafting a classroom lesson around this particular critical-creativity experience

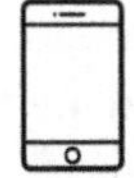
Experience involves mobile technology

Experience involves taking notes, sketching, doodling, or composing

Experience involves music whether creating, recording, listening or curating

Experience involves interacting with and/or collaborating with people

Experience involves Oreo cookies

Experience involves creating with modeling clay

Catalog entries focused on interpersonal critical-creativity experiences

Experience involves reading or creating text

Experience involves outdoor spaces

Experience involves recording audio

Experience may involve painting

Experience involves creating remixes of some sort

Experience involves paper, whether note taking, sketching, doodling or composing

Catalog entries with science applications

Experience involves scissors (naturally)

Experience involves tape

Catalog entries focused on social media critical-creativity experiences

What students can be expected to create, the tools they will use, and the essential critical-thinking skills being assessed by the entry's exercise

Catalog entries with social studies applications

Experience involves building with physical tools and materials

Experience involves listening to audio, whether musical, oral, or environmental

Experience involves watching or creating video

Experience involves sticky notes for organization, creation, or collaboration

Catalog entries with visual and performing arts applications

Catalog entries focused on physical material critical-creativity experiences

Catalog entries focused on word-based creativity experiences

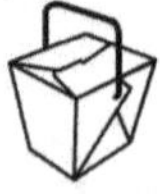
Highlights the higher-order thinking and bigger-picture understandings students will develop

Catalog entries with world language applications

CATALOG OF CRITICAL CREATIVITY:

CREATING WITH WORDS

Potent Quotables

Résumé Rationale

Line and Caret

Style Hack

Phrankenword

Blackout Poetry

Found Typoetry

CREATIVITY IS
INTELLIGENCE
HAVING FUN
ALBERT
EINSTEIN

Potent Quotables

#IntentionQuotes

60 minutes

TARGET

Create a thought-provoking, inspiring, or otherwise meaningful visual for social media by using principles of composition and graphic design to fuse a powerful quote with a purposeful image.

Potent Quotables asks students to interpret key quotations from notable figures and to demonstrate the depth of their understanding through visual representation for an audience.

PATHWAY

1. Provide students with a selection of three to five powerful, pithy, and meaningful quotations related to the current content. Limiting the selection provides opportunity for students to see how their peers problem solve and also makes for a more time-efficient activity.

2. Ask students to identify a quote that speaks to them and that they believe carries a message others should receive. It may be helpful for them to note, jot, doodle, or record their interpretations at this stage.

3. Direct students to a collection of Creative Commons Zero images online, such as Unsplash or Pexels. Images with a Creative Commons Zero license can be used for any purpose without attribution, though students should be encouraged to give credit regardless.

4. Ask students to find an image in the collection that illustrates their chosen quote.

5. Model a number of effective text and image combinations from social media sources, such as Instagram, Facebook, and Pinterest. Encourage students to use these examples as mentor images.

A. Familiarize students with designer Robin Williams' CRAP graphic design principles:

Contrast	Alignment
Repetition	Proximity

B. Familiarize students with photographer Joni James' composition principles:

Perspective	Decisive Moment
Inclusion	Leading Lines
Exclusion	Find a Frame
Movement	Rule of Thirds

6. Work with students to analyze one or two of the example visuals, focusing on how the text design (font, size, color, placement, etc.) works with the photo composition (subject, color, perspective, etc.) to enhance the meaning of both the words and the image.
7. Direct students to use an image editor, such as Google Drawings or Pixlr, to add the quote to their found image in a way that accurately represents their interpretation of the quotation, while looking like an image others would want to share.
8. Conduct small-group or whole-class critique sessions in which students share their intentions behind their designs and receive feedback.
9. Provide an opportunity for students to apply their feedback.
10. Share student images via the classroom and/or school social media accounts. Encourage students to share via their personal accounts as well.

TAKEAWAY

By creating social media-ready visuals from key quotations and found images, Potent Quotables requires students to understand key content while demonstrating intentional design skills. Students must establish relationships between the various design elements in their visuals (font, color, image, etc.) and the meaning of the quote. Critiques challenge students to evaluate the effectiveness of their choices, while publishing their work exposes them to the experience of creating for an authentic audience.

APPLICATION

Social Studies Use quotes from leaders of the civil rights movement, primary-source documents from the framers of the Constitution of the United States, or memoirs written by international youth activists.

Science Use quotes from scientists and innovators, acceptance speeches from Nobel Prize winners, or Newton's Laws of Motion.

World Languages Use lines of poetry or lyrics from the target language or use images from the target country of origin in conjunction with lines of poetry or lyrics from the students' first languages.

AMPLIFICATION

- Use student photography rather than found images. Add the creative constraint of taking images within the school or classroom to challenge further divergent thinking.
- Analyze the number of shares, views, likes, and interactions (the social media "reach") the images receive. Discuss with students why they think certain images catch on more than others.
- Conduct research prior to creating the visuals. Discover what types of images, colors, fonts, and other design elements appeal to the target audience for these images—other students, teachers, and parents. Challenge students to appeal to each specific audience's needs with their designs.

John Steinbeck, *Of Mice and Men*

Wallace Stevens, *The Snow Man*

John Steinbeck, *Of Mice and Men*

Résumé Rationale

#IntentionResume

45 minutes

TARGET

Create a résumé for a rule, principle, or law that proves it is well qualified to solve the problem at hand.

Résumé rationale asks students to identify the key features of a rule, principle, or law and then apply that knowledge to a problem-solving context.

PATHWAY

1. Share a number of sample résumés with students. Ask them to note the common features of a résumé, i.e., skills and qualifications, work history, and contact information.

2. Present students with one or more problems that need solving.

3. Ask students to adopt the role of one of the rules, principles, or laws currently being studied in class.

4. Instruct students to consider this rule, principle, or law unemployed and looking for work. The current problem at hand might just be what that rule, principle, or law needs to get on its feet again.

5. Provide time for students to design résumés from the point of view of their given rules, principles, or laws. Encourage them to think in puns and other forms of wordplay to demonstrate complete understanding of the concepts. Thus, the commutative property of addition might live at 1+A+B=B+A+1 Lane, while the Newton's First Law of Motion might have no permanent address (because it is always moving).

6. Conduct job interviews with the "applicant pool" about their qualifications for the task at hand. Students may then also record an audition reel or write a justification of the skills evident on the résumé.

TAKEAWAY

By creating lists of qualities and attributes and applying them to purposeful contexts, résumé rationale better ensures students have working knowledge of the rules, principles, and laws of a particular content area. Students must make accurate predictions and defend their understanding of the concept as it applies to solving a problem.

APPLICATION

Science Put Newton's Laws of Motion, simple machines, or properties of light, electricity, and heat to work solving everyday household problems.

Social Studies Present a new country looking for an economic system to adopt, a court case in need of a ruling, or a national problem that needs one of the branches of government to address.

Mathematics Present a series of construction needs that require particular geometric designs, a number of movie-theater management challenges that require mathematical operations, or a collection of personal finance questions that require algebraic properties.

AMPLIFICATION

- Share sample cover letters with students and ask them to make a cover letter from the point of view of their rule, principle, or law.
- Generate mock LinkedIn profiles for the rules, principles, or laws. (See Fauxial Media, page 292.)
- Organize a series of job interviews with in-depth role-play and a hiring committee comprising experts (teachers, students, parents, community members) in the problem and the principles.

Line and Caret

#IntentionLessAndMore

30 minutes

TARGET

Alter a word and give it new context by making as few changes as possible, either by adding letters with an editor's "caret" or removing them with a line.

Line and Caret is a form of wordplay that inspires students to consider dichotomies and think conceptually. Students are challenged to work within self-imposed creative constraints. It is a bit of a game to see how little can be changed to produce the greatest impact. If used as the #lessandmore activity, the emphasis is on reflection and articulation of an opinion—that is, what do we want to see "less of" and "more of"?

PATHWAY

1. Ask students to get into pairs, facing each other.

2. **Round 1: Opposites (Three minutes)** Explain that one person will say a word with a ***negative*** connotation (nouns and verbs work best, but they may be abstract or concrete). The partner should respond with a word that could mean the ***opposite*** or at least something ***more positive*** in nature. Encourage students to use sophisticated vocabulary and go beyond "black/white," "hot/cold."

3. **Round 2: Rhyming Opposites (Three to five minutes)** For this round, one person starts with a word with a negative connotation but one they think might not be too difficult to rhyme. The partner must then respond with a rhyming word that has a positive connotation. For example, "crying/trying," "teasing/pleasing," "hate/create."

4. Ask pair groups to partner with another pair. In groups of four, ask students to draw a line down the middle of a piece of large paper. Provide the prompt: ***What things frustrate you***

most? What are things in the world you think need changing? What bothers you about school/life/the world? What would you like to see less of?

5. They should then conduct a quick-think (about five minutes) and record as many ***negative words or short phrases*** as they can think of on one side of the paper. It helps to have one scribe and the other students providing the ideas.

6. Ask students to review the words. Are there any that can be changed slightly, either by adding or taking away letters, to form a more positive word or phrase? Are there any that have a rhyming word or phrase that would have a more positive connotation? Solicit examples from the groups. NOTE: Challenge students to ***forge relationships between the words,*** so that they make sense together, e.g., "doubt/do," "insanity/humanity," "dreary/dreamy."

7. Tell students to use the other side of the paper to write some of the word remixes. There should be active discussion in the group. NOTE: If students get stuck in this phase, ask them to flip the process and first think of some positive concepts they would like to see more of, and then change them to the negative.

8. Distribute index cards or larger paper and ask each student to draw a word combination, using the caret mark or line symbols. Encourage them to play with color and typography. Each student should do at least one word remix, though if groups have generated more ideas, they may draw them all.

9. Students should share their word remixes with the class at large and offer offer their reasoning behind their choices. Ask them to share why these concepts are important to them and what impact this change would make if implemented.

10. Display the cards as a grid in the classroom, as they are quite effective when seen together as a collection.

11. If students maintain blogs or digital portfolios, ask them to take pictures of their work and then write or record their explanations.

TAKEAWAY

Students should come away with an appreciation of the fragility and malleable nature of language as they play with making small changes to words that in turn create a significant impact. They may see how simple messages can reveal great truths or challenge viewers to think about grand concepts ***(media literacy)***. This is a ***metacognitive*** exercise in which students have a chance to explore and share their feelings about change and the things that bother them or delight them. Experimenting with remix and playing with dichotomies help students hone their ***creative-thinking skills*** as they see how recombination influences creative work.

APPLICATION

Visual and Performing Arts Students may act out the #lessandmore concepts or use them as inspiration for song-lyric writing. Visual artists may create works that embed the word remixes into their work, play with typography, or make a guerrilla art campaign.

Health and Physical Education Emphasize the less/more in relation to personal health and fitness. Students may create word remixes based on their content knowledge (nutrition, exercise, healthful habits, etc.) and develop posters or public service announcements.

World Language Students can practice their target language using this exercise, which gets them thinking about meaning, context, and nuance of the vocabulary, as well as word structure.

AMPLIFICATION

- Students may illustrate their word remixes in any number of ways: on the index card itself, as a poster, or as a photo with typographic overlay, for example.
- If students have a drawing app, they might digitally draw their word remix, which can then be shared on social media.

- Compile the word remixes into a short film, or ask the students to hold their cards up as you film or photograph each one in order to create a digital story.
- Play a game in which students exchange words generated by the class in the initial quick-think (this could be drawn from a hat). Each student is then challenged to alter the given word in one or more ways, as long as the context is changed.
- If the class is connected to another class virtually, they may volley the words back and forth in a remix collaboration.
- Alter the #lessandmore challenge by asking students to provide two rhyming words in the following template: "less plan, more play" or "less testing, more questing."

mus~~t~~ [e]

pla~~n~~ [y]

dou~~b~~t

te[a]ch

Style Hack

#IntentionStyleHack

120 minutes

TARGET

Use an alternative genre of media—whether print, visual, audio, video, social, or a combination of the above—to demonstrate understanding of key concepts from a lesson or unit of study.

Style Hack asks students to filter through a different genre in order to demonstrate understanding of nuances and motifs.

The juxtaposition is often anachronistic and can be created by various media, such as visual art, memes, films, social media accounts, text, and audio.

PATHWAY

1. Students should be able to identify an aspect of the course content they would like to use as a subject. This could be a ***real or fictitious person*** (such as a well-known scientist or literary character), ***an event*** (such as a war or discovery), a ***creative work*** (such as a poem, film, novel, or painting), or ***a concept*** (nuclear energy, a sport, or a philosophy).

2. Help students prepare by discussing which subjects would be appropriate. It might be that this exercise is structured around a particular aspect of the content at a given time (such as a poet you are studying). However, Style Hack can be a useful culminating project at the ***end of a learning period***. Students could brainstorm as a class and generate a list of potential subjects.

3. Once students choose their subjects, they should spend some time creating a mind map of traits specific to that subject. People and literary figures are perhaps the most obvious in their mannerisms, voices, looks, habits, and motivations. If analyzing a creative work, students should identify components of style.

Break an event into mini-events, causes, parties involved, and results. Students should attempt to ***personify*** a concept and generate ideas as to how that can be articulated through image and text.

4. Students then choose a style hack, or the genre that they will use to filter the subject. Ideally, the class may brainstorm a list of possible genres. Challenge students to think about connections they can make between the two. For example, a "moody" poet could be translated into a sullen indie rock star; monarchs could have LinkedIn pages; a political philosophy could be transformed into a Twitter feed.

Suggestions

Pop It! Make anything "pop culture." Make references to current television shows and films, music styles and artists, fashion trends, etc.

Anachronism Place the subject in a different time period. When historical subjects in particular are re-contextualized, students often gain empathy for the characters involved.

Social Media (Faux Facebook, Snapchat, Instagram, or Twitter parody account) Students really need to "get inside the head" of their subject in order to create a nuanced social media presence. Most students are familiar with how these spaces are negotiated, so it is helpful to brainstorm some common attributes with the class (for example, specific hashtags used like #tbt, #fbf, or #nofilter). It is helpful to offer some exemplars of existing parody accounts to critique.

Twitter Chat/Backchannel Use Twitter or the more private TodaysMeet (todaysmeet.com) to conduct an "in-character" chat. Each student should assume a role of an individual pertinent to the course (literary figures, famous scientists, artists, or rulers, participants in an event, chemical elements, geometric shapes, etc.). Run the chat asynchronously or synchronously, and develop questions and guidelines with students prior to the exercise.

Children's Book Hack Ask students to choose a well-known children's book—perhaps a beloved one from their own childhood experience. You might want to gather some examples from the school library or ask students to bring in a few from home. Students should choose a book or style and develop their own version, based on the selected course content. The aesthetic and text style should remain true to the original, but the content gives it new meaning. It is more effective if there is some correlation between the two, such as in **Ruben Bolling's Richard Scarry *Busytown* remix about Silicon Valley**. (See also: Dick and Jane: Jedi Masters; Faux Little Golden Books)

Yearbook Most students are familiar with yearbook formats and in particular, the "Senior" section highlighting individual students. Ask students to imagine their chosen content as being a featured student in the school yearbook. In addition to an image, they may think of aspirations, memories, quotes, advice, nicknames, favorite classes, and other common elements.

Use at least half of the time allotted for thinking and planning. Devote the other half for making and presenting (except in the case of the backchannel activity). Students should clearly articulate their creative reasoning and in what ways their knowledge of the content is evident in their remix. If students maintain blogs or digital portfolios, ask them to take pictures of their work and then write or record their explanations.

TAKEAWAY

Students should come away with an appreciation of how remix and parody might provide an added commentary on the subject ***(media literacy)***. They should understand the essence of the content enough to be able to re-contextualize it ***(creative and critical thinking)***. They should have cultivated empathy for the subject and predict how that subject might "act" if placed in a different context. In remixing, they may draw parallels between their lives and environment and those of the subject ***(metacognition)***.

APPLICATION

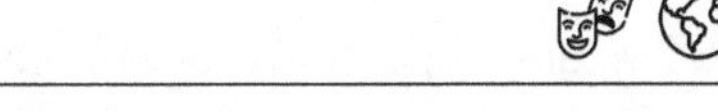

Visual and Performing Arts Students can create and perform a parody song or rap based on their selected content. Content filtered through a popular television show or film style may be performed live. Students may develop social media profiles for famous artists or create children's book hacks for art movements.

Social Studies Historical figures easily lend themselves to parody social media accounts. Events can be "backchanneled" as a Twitter chat. Concepts, like political movements or philosophies, can be re-contextualized as fashion lines or explained in the form of a children's book.

Science Students can personify concepts, such as the periodic table of elements or gravity, or assume the roles of famous scientists and interact in social media accounts or other pop-culture expressions.

 AMPLIFICATION

- Students creating a children's book hack may read their remix (if appropriate) to a class of younger children or perhaps make a video version of the book with a voiceover of their reading.

- Creating parody accounts on social media platforms allows others to collaborate in the new digital identities of these characters. Followers can respond to posts with additions of their own, participating in the development of the character, and often offering insights. Why not collaborate with another class outside your geographical area?

- For a Twitter chat, create a designated hashtag and advertise the chat on social media. Invite other schools or anyone who might have interest to participate. Archive the chat in storify.com for further amplification.

- For any of the projects, students may use digital storytelling tools (such as photography and film) to create content that can be easily shared across various platforms. Some of the ideas lend themselves to becoming posters that can be displayed around campus.

- If students create poetry, songs, or raps, host a "poetry slam" featuring student performances.

- Some entrepreneurial-minded students might create a product line, bringing their chosen content into pop culture. They can prototype their products with photo-editing tools and build a website showcasing them (recommended: wix.com).

Phrankenword

#IntentionWord

45 minutes

TARGET

Create a brand-new word by mashing up two or more vocabulary terms. Provide a definition and use that new word to tell a story.

Phrankenword asks students to define key vocabulary and then apply that knowledge to the development of original terms for familiar and unfamiliar contexts.

PATHWAY

1. Ask students to re-familiarize themselves with their current vocabulary terms if they have not done so. Consider using self-paced, formative assessment tools, such as Google Form or Quizlet, to facilitate this work.

2. Distribute index cards to students, enough for students to create a deck of flashcards without the definitions.

3. Model a "phrankenword" for students by mashing up two words from different subject matters and defining the new term. This is traditionally known as a "***portmanteau***" (French for a valise, due to its two parts coming together as one). For example, "evaporation" and "condensation" might be mashed up into "evapensation," a noun meaning the water droplets that form on the underside of a surface suspended over a water source. Note: DO NOT show students an example using their current words. It is okay for them to be messy in this thinking.

4. (Clock icon w/ less than sign?) **Three minutes.** Make as many phrankenwords as you can in the next three minutes. Remember that you can use more than one word. Use the cards to physically move the words around, lay them over one another, or criss-cross them. Also feel free to note, jot, and doodle on scrap paper, or on the cards themselves. Keep track of the words you create.

5. Conduct a Think-Pair-Share. Ask students to define three of their phrankenwords, establishing parts of speech and meaning based on the meaning of the original word.
   - "Pair up with a partner and share your phrankenwords. Be certain to share the roots of that phrankenword and your current definition."
   - "Choose one phrankenword from each partner to share with the class."
   - "Share out. Take note of any phrankenword you hear that sounds interesting to you."
6. Pose the creative constraints for this challenge.
   - Tell a story with a beginning, a middle, and an end.
   - Use any storytelling medium (audio, video, image, print) to tell the story or any combination of the above.
   - Use the phrankenword as the part of speech to which it belongs.
   - Use context clues to help unfamiliar readers understand what the phrankenword means.
7. Conduct a gallery walk or showcase of the phrankenword stories, including student critiques and explanations of intentions.

TAKEAWAY

By creating new words from key vocabulary, phrankenwords reinforce student understanding of the source terms, while building capacity for divergent thinking. To construct a phrankenword, students must first analyze the origins (etymology) of current vocabulary and be intentional as they remix syllables and roots, prefixes, and suffixes. Storytelling requires students apply their knowledge to new circumstances in a way that makes sense to an audience.

APPLICATION

Science Engineer a genus and species of animal, discover an element on the periodic table, or register a phenomenon of weather.

Social Studies Rename a country based on its governmental structure, religious profile, and economic system. Advertise a political candidate from the past or present, a controversial law or policy, or a nation's tourism industry.

Mathematics Design a new geometric shape by mashing up two or more existing forms, create a new unit of measurement for a specific task, or establish a new mathematical operation.

AMPLIFICATION

- Use the phrankenword to explain a concept.
- Use the phrankenword to solve a problem.
- Distribute the advertisements online or in print form to reach both the intended audience as well as others who may find delight and joy in seeing the students' creativity.
- Teach students the three classical forms of appeal: character (ethos), emotion (pathos), and reason (logos). Have them apply one or more of those forms to their advertisement.
- Publish the advertisements and interview a "focus group" about their effectiveness, just as an advertising agency would do. Apply the feedback and create new iterations.
- Adjust your audience from next year's students to this year's parents and guardians. This can be a powerful way for students to build empathy for their parents and guardians, while engaging the folks at home in their students' thinking.
- Shifting the task from "advertise" to "illustrate" opens up more possibilities while keeping the benefits of divergent thinking intact. Apply this challenge to any content or concept in any classroom.

Blackout Poetry

#IntentionBlackout

60 minutes

TARGET

Create a poem from a selection of text by crossing out words and lines, leaving the reader with an original work that reveals deeper understanding of the original text.

Blackout Poetry asks students to distill key words from a text and then present those ideas in an original poetic composition that reveals insights about the text's deeper meaning or theme.

PATHWAY

1. Ask students to familiarize themselves with a brief article, excerpt, or primary-source document.
2. Distribute an index card to each student.
3. Instruct students to note, jot, or doodle key words, phrases, and/or lines from the text onto the index card. Provide the creative constraint that they may only fill a single side of the card with their notes, jots, or doodles.
4. Model a "blackout poem" for students.
    - Distribute and display copies of a related article, excerpt, or primary-source document. Avoid using the same text as the students to encourage creative and unique solutions.
    - Note, jot, or doodle key words, phrases, and/or lines from the text on an index card.
    - Consider which of those key words, phrases, and/or lines are essential to the text.
    - Use a marker to cross out all of the other words on the original document.
    - Continue crossing out words to create a poetic arrangement of words, phrases, and lines that reveals insights about the text's deeper meaning or theme.

5. Challenge students to create their own blackout poems from the provided text. Be prepared with multiple copies of the original texts until students grow their creative confidence.

6. Ask students to document the intention behind their blackout poems by taking pictures of their work and then writing or recording their explanations.

TAKEAWAY

By creating a poem from the language and structure of a source text, blackout poetry asks students to distill meaning while constructing, arranging, and juxtaposing ideas. Students learn to prioritize as they must choose which words to retain and which to eliminate. They establish new relationships between one part of the text and another, while making sense of the text as a whole.

APPLICATION

Science Distill editorials regarding climate change, endangered species, or space exploration to reveal the cores of the authors' intentions.

Health and Physical Education Blackout a recipe to reveal the technique, flavors, and textures that make that dish unique from others. Blackout ingredient labels and nutritional information from food packaging to share a poem of eating habits.

World Language After students compose and perform original dialogues, instruct them to blackout the script to reveal the nature of the relationship between the two characters. Challenge them to continue revising their dialogues until the relationship is evident in both the dialogue and the blackout poetry.

AMPLIFICATION

- Apply a satirical or ironic lens to the readings and ask students to uncover the hidden meanings in the text. What might an editorial about gun control or the warranty for a new cell phone really be saying?

- Use digital tools such as Google Docs or Google Drawing to create digital blackout poetry. Massachusetts-based digital-learning specialist Kerry Gallagher (@KerryHawk02) has done exceptional work with students making digital blackout poems out of primary-source historical documents.
- Experiment with white-out, rubber cement, and graphite to create erasure poems. Cover over a text in one of those three mediums, and then reveal poetry in its lines by peeling back the top layer. This can create a more tactile experience for students.

IN CONGRESS, July 4, 1776.

The unanimous Declaration of the thirteen united States of America,

When in the Course of human events, it becomes necessary for one people to dissolve the political bands which have connected them with another, and to assume among the powers of the earth, the separate and equal station to which the Laws of Nature and of Nature's God entitle them, a decent respect to the opinions of mankind requires that they should declare the causes which impel them to the separation.

We hold these truths to be self-evident, that all men are created equal, that they are endowed by their Creator with certain unalienable Rights, that among these are Life, Liberty and the pursuit of Happiness.--That to secure these rights, Governments are instituted among Men, deriving their just powers from the consent of the governed, --That whenever any Form of Government becomes destructive of these ends, it is the Right of the People to alter or to abolish it, and to institute new Government, laying its foundation on such principles and organizing its powers in such form, as to them shall seem most likely to effect their Safety and Happiness. Prudence, indeed, will dictate that Governments long established should not be changed for light and transient causes; and accordingly all experience hath shewn, that mankind are more disposed to suffer, while evils are sufferable, than to right themselves by abolishing the forms to which they are accustomed. But when a long train of abuses and usurpations, pursuing invariably the same Object evinces a design to reduce them under absolute Despotism, it is their right, it is their duty, to throw off such Government, and to provide new Guards for their future security.--Such has been the patient sufferance of these Colonies; and such is now the necessity which constrains them to alter their former Systems of Government. The history of the present King of Great Britain is a history of repeated injuries and usurpations, all having in direct object the establishment of an absolute Tyranny over these States. To prove this, let Facts be submitted to a candid world.

Found TyPoetry

#IntentionFoundTyPoetry

60 minutes

TARGET

Use various examples of typography/fonts from the environment to create a poem or poetic phrase.

While there are numerous styles and processes to create found poetry, this version gives students the opportunity to interact with their environments as they hunt for examples of typography in signage. They use photography to capture the visual artifacts and piece words and letters together to spell out their poem.

PATHWAY

1. If students have access to computers, ask each to type a sentence in their favorite font. (Iideally, they could each type their name in their chosen font on a shared document.) Lead the class in a short discussion about why they are drawn to that particular font. Ask them to think about the "personality" of the font and what sort of feeling it elicits. Alternatively, create a short slide deck of typography examples (either fonts or found type from signage) and solicit opinions from the students.

2. *Metaphorical typography exercise:* Distribute index cards and ask students to write a vocabulary term from your course on one side of the card. Students may then exchange cards with a partner and attempt to create metaphorical typography with the word. They should try to write the word with a lettering that visually depicts the meaning of the word (such as a frozen-looking "ice" or the word "wall" with letters comprised of "bricks"). Allow about five minutes for this, and then ask students to share their examples with the class. They should explain their creative reasoning.

3. Explain to students that they will be going on a "hunt" for words in their environment. They will seek out examples of typography on signs, buildings, and objects (the "environment" may be the neighborhood, a field-trip destination, or the school itself). Their goal is to take photos

of interesting words and/or letters that they can then use to create poetry. Note: They may also wish to capture ***objects that look like letters***, such as a window that resembles a "t." They should aim for at least twenty images.

4. Designate a time period for the typography scavenger hunt. This could be a part of the class period, though it could also be assigned as an off-campus activity and continued the following meeting.

5. After students return with the images, advise them to place all the photos in a space where they can easily see them all at a glance and manipulate them (e.g., they could print them out or view their photo library as a grid).

6. Challenge students to compose a poem or poetic phrase with the found typography, ideally relating to your course content. Encourage them to consider the tone of the type—that is, can the feelings elicited by the lettering help convey the intent of the poem?

7. Students may create one or more poems to share with the class. They should find a way to display them visually by arranging them with a digital collage tool, building a slide deck, or printing them.

8. Ask students to document the intention behind their found typography poems by writing or recording their explanations.

TAKEAWAY

Students practice ***mindfulness*** as they take notice of their surrounding environment and capture typographic elements. They gain understanding of the "feel" of a font and how design affects message. Working within the ***creative constraint*** of "found" source material requires students to see new relationships and construct meaning from concrete rather than abstract design. They see that a traditionally text-based creation can be enhanced by other mediums such as photography.

APPLICATION

World Languages Build words in the target language from individual letters spliced together to create words. They can write poetry, perhaps be required to form a specific sentence structure, or include one of their current vocabulary words. For added grammar practice, they can each form a word from the found typography, print it out, add it to a crowdsourced word bank, and play with remixing them into logical phrases.

ELA Use quotes from authors, poets, or novels as inspiration, or create a response to an existing line found in a book, play, or poem. Of course, original poetry is always a plus—perhaps add a constraint like a particular theme.

Visual and Performing Arts Act out the found word and shoot a video or make a GIF from a series of photos. Alternatively, ask visual-arts students to create a piece of artwork that relates to their found word poem, so that the poem becomes the caption or title.

AMPLIFICATION

- Instead of students creating a poem from their own images, ask students to pool together images and develop a word bank from which all students may draw. (A shared digital folder works well for this, or the images could be printed.) Each student then composes a poem from the crowdsourced collection of typographic artifacts.
- Try a collaborative poem. Students could pair up, form small groups, or even write a class poem using the words they collect.
- Remix one another's poems by exchanging and rearranging. Alternatively, mashups may be created by mixing individual poems.
- Create an animated GIF using a digital GIF-making tool (Amy recommends ImgPlay for iOS). The stop-motion movie technique (a series of images at a quick speed) can also be used for this. Share to social media sites as a video.

DRAWING IS
PUTTING
A LINE
AROUND
AN
IDEA
HENRI
MATISSE

CATALOG OF CRITICAL CREATIVITY: CREATING WITH IMAGES

Color Palette

#IntentionColor

45 minutes

TARGET

Design a custom color palette to demonstrate an understanding of the central themes in a text.

Color Palette asks students to identify the theme of a text based on available evidence and represent that thinking through a collection of custom-selected, custom-named colors. Students must apply metaphorical thinking, descriptive language, and wordplay to effectively convey meaning through a title and a color.

PATHWAY

1. Bring a number of paint chips to class and ask students to work in groups of two or three to come up with a new three-color scheme for the classroom. They should be prepared to justify their choices.
2. Facilitate a series of quick pitches in which groups make the case for the new color scheme in the room and vote on a winning scheme.
3. As a class, collaborate on new names for the three colors, names that better represent the atmosphere of the classroom, i.e., "Empathetic Blue," "Collaboration Gray," and "Always Another Opportunity Eggshell."
4. Determine two layers of reasoning for those new color names: one for the new name and one for why ***that*** color should receive that name. For example, Empathetic Blue represents the empathy we use in this room to connect with one another. Blue is also a soothing color that we associate with waves and water, just like the waves of calm that come when we empathize with one another.
5. Set the color schemes aside for a few minutes and turn attention to the class's current text.
6. Conduct a Think-Pair-Share around the themes and big ideas evident in the text.

- Use a blank piece of paper and create a word cluster in the middle of themes and big ideas the text suggests.

- Add evidence in the form of characters, plot events, setting, conflicts, etc. toward the outer edges of the paper, drawing lines to link the evidence and themes.

- Pair with a partner and examine and add new ideas to one another's maps.

- Choose a single theme and evidence to share with the rest of class.

7. After the theme share, direct students toward ColourLovers.com, a free color palette and design tool. Provide them a few minutes to play with the site.

8. Challenge students to create a three-color palette for the text based on these creative constraints.

9. Each color must receive a unique name based on the two layers of intention described above.

10. The three colors must work together as a collection, both in terms of how they look (aesthetics) and what they mean (substance).

11. The intentions behind each color must be written or recorded with evidence.

12. Conduct a gallery walk or showcase of the color palettes, including student critiques and explanations of intentions.

TAKEAWAY

Color Palette promotes layers of critical thinking. Choosing colors challenges students to analyze the impact colors have upon viewers. Naming the colors requires that students have a working knowledge of themes present and articulate that knowledge in a succinct way. Establishing a complete color scheme—not just allowing a random selection of colors—asks students to think in terms of systems and relationships.

APPLICATION

Science Colorize each stage of a process, such as the water cycle or cellular reproduction, each category of a taxonomy, such as the animal kingdom or the periodic table of elements, or each item in a collection, such as the planets or the continents.

Social Studies Choose colors for maps of the states or provinces, charts that document the passage of major explorers, or infographics illustrating voting results from a community.

Mathematics Design a palette for the order of mathematical operations, the classification of geometric shapes, or a set of functions.

AMPLIFICATION

- Create a thematic piece of artwork using the intentional color palette.
- Load the color palette into Google Docs by using the hex codes available on ColourLovers.com. Then mark up a selection from a text, related article, or student writing using the colors as highlights to indicate thematic or conceptual connections.
- Grow the color palettes over a series of units, building more and more layers of intentionality and evolving into a system of color.
- After creating the first palette, investigate color theory and psychology. Revise the palette to align with the research into traditional color meanings.

Two Images, One Question

#Intention2i1Q

60 minutes

TARGET

Create a three-slide presentation that uses two images and a single open-ended question to demonstrate deep understanding of a research topic.

Two Images, One Question presentations rely on students practicing effective research and inquiry techniques, while using visuals to take the place of written summaries or paraphrases of that research. Students must identify appropriate fair-use images that serve as metaphors or analogies for the content. Students must determine the most essential information to share with their peers and craft open-ended questions that leave other students thinking about why this information matters.

PATHWAY

1. Warm up by exploring evocative, metaphorical images. Post several photos around the room that could be symbolic of something in your curriculum. Ask students to think about what analogies they can make with what they have studied and the respective images. It might be helpful to post ". . . is like_______" under each photo. Allow about ten minutes for students to post sticky notes or, if the image is posted on a whiteboard or poster, write their ideas directly underneath. This exercise can also be done in a digital space using whatever platform you are comfortable with that allows for posting of images and crowdsourced text responses.

2. Discuss the labels students assigned to the photos. ***What made them think in the ways they did? Why are metaphorical images more powerful than more literal interpretations?***

3. Introduce the challenge. Students will be asked to conduct research in the content area (such as reading a piece of text or an article or viewing a video). The goal is to develop a succinct and engaging short presentation in order to teach peers—in other words, they will be the "experts" on this specific topic. The creative constraint is a total of three slides presenting two images and one open-ended question that will prompt a class discussion.

4. Reiterate the distinction between ***closed-*** and ***open-ended*** questions. Open-ended questions draw upon feelings, personal experiences, and opinions rather than facts. They require detailed explanations and thoughtful answers, often opening the discussion up to multiple perspectives. Some open-ended questions require the creative-thinking practice of making predictions, such as ***"What would happen if . . .?"*** While closed questions result in a simple "yes" or "no" answer, open-ended questions use wording that invites scenarios and anecdotes. Practice developing open-ended questions in partner groups. Partners can choose one or two of the following categories and inquire about their peer's daily life or personal history.

Considering consequences: *What would happen if you . . . ?*

Comparing and Contrasting: *How are ___ the same or different?*

Making Predictions: *What do you think will happen if . . . ?*

Affective Inquiry: *How do you feel about . . . ? In your opinion . . . ? What do you think of . . . ?*

Evaluating Reasoning: *What made you decide to . . . ? Why do you think . . . ?*

Extending Thinking: *How would this be different if . . . ?*

Exploring Solutions: *How would you solve the problem of . . . ?*

TAKEAWAY

Two Images, One Question challenges students to apply metaphorical thinking and effective question techniques to inform and engage an audience. Students must synthesize the results of their research into a short visual presentation, preparing them for the more visual world of communication in which we now live. Developing powerful questions demonstrates not only student understanding of the research topic but also the relevance of that research to others' lives. Further, as students choose the images for their presentations, they must find Creative Commons licensed images or create images of their own, reinforcing the importance of attribution, creative confidence, and making digital media that is ready to be shared with a wider audience.

APPLICATION

Science Conduct research on the latest findings in a particular aspect of a certain topic area (for example, with the topic "neuroscience," students could research brain development, memory, neuromarketing, learning theory, etc.). As the "expert" for that subtopic, teach the class about the main findings as expressed in the readings or video. Choose strong metaphorical images that guide the oral presentation and further the understanding of a complex idea. Pose open-ended questions that may not have a definitive answer, but incite curiosity and critical thinking in the other students.

World Languages Read an article or watch a video in the target language and develop a Two Image, One Question presentation accordingly. Practice impromptu dialogue as you lead the class in the discussion around the open-ended question. Or, research the etymology of a word or the origins of an idiomatic phrase. Use this structure to share with the class and ask volunteers to use it in an original sentence in the target language.

Mathematics Present about "math in the real world." Use two images that depict a certain formula, theorem, or other math principle as they occur in the natural and physical world. Develop a question prompt about what kinds of problems could be solved using this formula, or imagine what would happen if the formula were applied to something else.

AMPLIFICATION

- Create a voiceover recording for the slide deck and export as a movie file. Upload to social media with a hashtag so that responses to the question might be archived.
- Design original images using student's own photography or artistic skills.
- Use the slide presentation tool Projeqt (projeqt.com) to create a dynamic presentation with the ability to included embedded Twitter and Instagram feeds. Challenge audience members to use these during the presentation, or draw from other crowdsourced material.
- Remix a traditional slide deck into this format. Often, presentations are simply "chalk and talk" and do not include a provocation for the audience. Convert a typical slide deck into a Two Image, One Question version.
- Hold a learning fair/presentation of knowledge festival event in which students have the chance to showcase their Two Image, One Question presentations.
- Make this style of research and presentation a routine in the course. Students can develop one for each unit or topic and curate in a blog space of their own.
- Younger students can do this without the use of digital technology. They can showcase their knowledge using bulletin boards or other wall space—perhaps in the main school corridor. They may make posters with annotated images describing key points and then pose the question. Passersby may interact by using sticky notes to record their answers.
- Use a backchannel, like Twitter or TodaysMeet (todaysmeet.com), during the Socratic discussion of the question prompt. Students can post text responses as well as participate in the live discussion.

Minimalist Poster

#IntentionMinimalism

60 minutes

TARGET

Illustrate a complex concept or idea by designing a minimalist poster.

Minimalist poster design requires students apply principles of minimalism such as monochromatic color palettes, basic geometric figures, and limited text, while considering how the arrangement and the number of shapes might create metaphorical meaning. Students must have accurate and in-depth content knowledge of the concept in order to develop visuals that are both straightforward and nuanced.

PATHWAY

1. Share the following quotes with students:

"Big ideas are usually simple ideas."

—David Ogilvy,
twentieth-century advertising giant

"Almost all quality of improvement comes via simplification of design . . . "

—Tom Peters,
twentieth-century businessman

"Simplicity is the ultimate sophistication."

—Leonardo da Vinci,
Renaissance artist and engineer

"The simplification of anything is always sensational."

—G.K. Chesterton,
twentieth-century writer and philosopher

"The best for the most for the least."

—Charles Eames,
twentieth-century designer

2. Ask students to comment on the quotes in their journals, in a Think-Pair-Share, or as a class discussion. Prompt them to think about the following: ***Why is simple better? What makes something "simple" (what do we mean by "simplicity")? How could one go about simplifying something? What kind of designs or things are simple yet effective, meaningful, and/or beautiful?***

3. Explain that there is a design movement called ***minimalism*** and an artistic practice called ***abstraction***. Both strip things down to the core and reduce things to their most essential elements. ***Abstraction*** is derived from the Latin, ***"to draw away from"*** and requires "drawing out" the most necessary components from unwanted detail. For example, an artist might use the most pared-down elements such as a limited or monochromatic color palette, solid-block fill, or basic geometric figures. There is little detail or flourish, and that is what makes the message so powerful. Older students can review the Wikipedia entry for Minimalism en.wikipedia.org/wiki/Minimalism for more background, or can be challenged to research a particular artist or designer's work in more depth.

4. Describe the goal of the challenge: to visually depict a complex idea in a minimalist way, yet still achieve communicating the meaning and one's understanding of it. Students can review the following for inspiration:

   - Atipo Design Firm, Minimalist Movie Posters: wired.com/2014/07/atipo-minimalist-movie-posters
   - Noma Bar, Guess Who? Cultural Icon Project: brainpickings.org/2011/07/28/noma-bar-guess-who/
   - Nick Barclay, Symptoms of Depression: bit.ly/depressionposters
   - Genis Carreras, Philographics (Philosophy posters): studiocarreras.com/philographics/

5. Guide the students in selecting the content they wish to explore. Prior to starting the visualization, they should jot down relevant characteristics, pieces of information, feelings, etc. that comprise the nuance of the subject. Color and symbolism comes into play here, and they might need to research these things further.

6. Encourage students to carefully consider the design elements they will use to construct the image. They might want to limit the color palette to two or three hues; they might want to use geometric or ultra-stylized figures (such as the ones found on street signs); or, they might think of a common theme they can use as a metaphor (like animals or candy); they might choose to use an unexpected medium like pasta or paint splatters.

7. Decide whether or not including text or titles is an option. Certainly, text should be limited to less than a sentence. In order to demonstrate their understanding, students should write or vlog about their considerations when developing the design for this content.

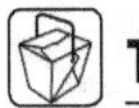

TAKEAWAY

Minimalist-poster design challenges students to experiment with a number of approaches to finding a seemingly simple solution to a complex problem. Students revisit their definitions of simplicity, discovering that layers of intention can be expressed in just a few shapes and colors. Effective minimalism requires deep and nuanced understanding of the subject matter, distilling essential qualities and uncovering unexpected, yet accessible, ways to capture them. Minimalist posters remind students that even the ordinary has potential to do powerful work.

CONFLICT

METAPHOR

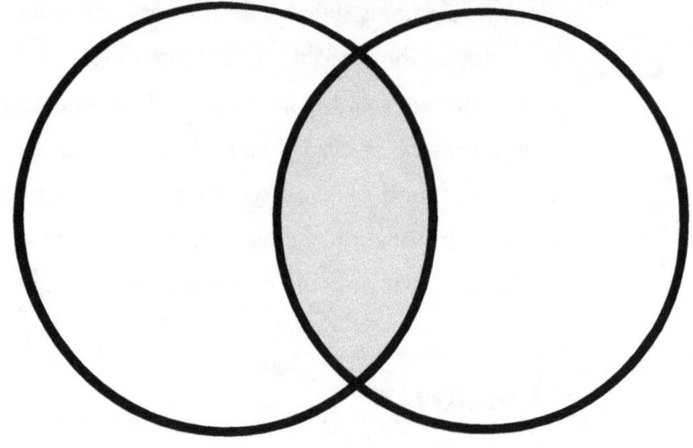

HUBRIS

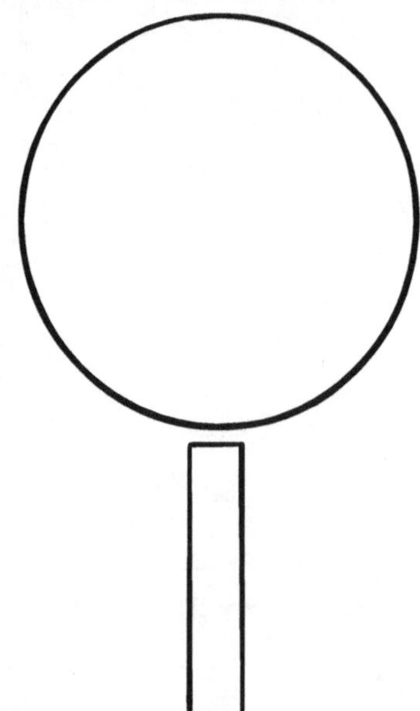

HYPERBOLE

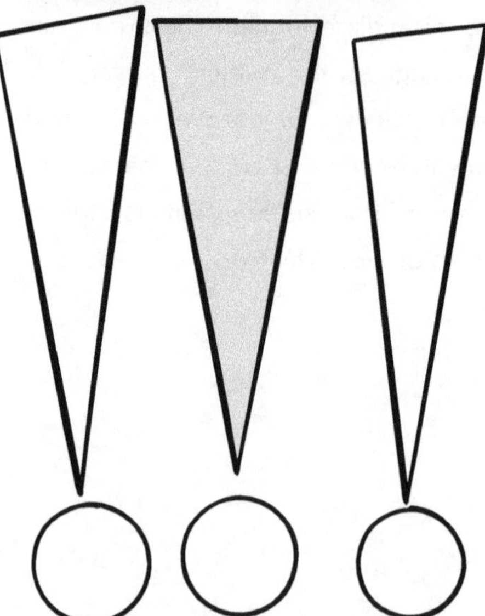

APPLICATION

ELA Design minimalist posters that symbolize literary devices. Use inspiration from this dichotomy project (bit.ly/2kindsofpeopleimages) to develop a series of posters that show the differences between two opposing literary characters or genres.

Social Studies Imagine a film adaptation of a historical event or biography of a historical figure's life. Using that concept, create the minimalist movie poster. Design posters to symbolize political theories, movements, or eras in history (for example, "communism," "social Darwinism," "The Great Leap Forward," or "The Renaissance").

Mathematics Use geometric figures only to depict something from either the math course or another course (such as an art movement or, in psychology, symptoms of a disorder). Illustrate a math principle, such as a theorem or formula, as a minimalist poster. Show "math in the real world" by using motifs from the environment that exemplify mathematical concepts (such as stylized pine trees for ***triangles*** or human figures for ***ratio***).

AMPLIFICATION

- Use three-dimensional materials to assemble the poster as a mixed-media collage or even transform them into a minimalist sculpture.
- Instead of designing one poster, develop an entire series built around a theme.
- Print posters on quality paper and post around campus or the local area. QR codes linked to videos, blogs, or other websites can be affixed in order to give the viewer more information.
- Upload the poster image to ThingLink (thinglink.com) and annotate with additional information.
- Assemble student posters in a digital gallery (website, epub, etc.) and share to social media channels.
- If using the minimalist posters as a "film poster," create a film trailer to go along with it.

Mondrian-ify

#IntentionMondrianify

60 minutes

TARGET

Use simple, abstract shapes and carefully chosen color palettes to create a visual story that demonstrates content-knowledge understanding in the modernist style of Dutch artist Piet Mondrian.

To Mondrian-ify one's learning, a student must identify the factual knowledge to include in the story and choose the colors and shapes that would best represent that knowledge. Students should consider the symbolic meanings of color and how the arrangement of simple shapes can convey complex ideas.

PATHWAY

1. As a warm-up, ask students to think about how their day is going. (If it is early in the day, they may rather recall the previous day.) Using a piece of paper and a pen or colored markers, ask them to try to depict the progression of their day using only lines, geometric shapes, space, and color (if available). Some things to consider: ***What activities did they participate in? What sorts of emotions did they have throughout the day? What was the weather like?*** Remind students to refrain from sketching recognizable objects—they should stick to abstract shapes and lines. After about five minutes, debrief by first asking some students to share their work and their reasoning (alternatively, students can share with a partner or small group). ***What was challenging about this activity? What shapes seemed like an obvious fit? Which items were more difficult to depict?***

2. Show some artwork from the Dutch artist Piet Mondrian. Depending on the age level of students, share some background into his style. One of the most famous is ***Composition with Large Red Plane, Yellow, Black, Gray, and Blue*** (1921). Share that this art style, called ***De Stijl,*** is all about reducing things to the essential elements. Mondrian said: ***"I wish to approach***

truth as closely as is possible, and therefore I abstract everything until I arrive at the fundamental quality of objects." Mondrian simplified everything to lines and shapes (mostly rectangles) and used a limited color palette (primary colors). Artist Pablo Picasso also believed in abstraction, and his iconic "Bull" series (artyfactory.com/art_appreciation/animals_in_art/pablo_picasso.htm) has been used to guide designers by demonstrating the beauty of simplistic, essential forms.

3. Present the challenge. Students should aim to translate a complex idea from the curriculum into a representative story using abstract shapes and a minimal color palette only. If text is allowed as part of the creative constraint, suggest using a maximum of one or two words. The stories can be created using a variety of mediums, including stop-motion animation, film, photography, collage, or sculpture.

4. Students should be given the opportunity to share their creations and explain the symbolism. Some might want to include a key in their write-up, indicating what the shapes and colors mean and why they chose them to illustrate a particular point.

TAKEAWAY

Mondrian-ify challenges students to use simplistic images and a limited color palette to relate complex ideas. Students discover the impact a single shape or splash of color may have on an audience, how an artist might use these tools to his or her advantage, and how big ideas can be expressed in simple ways. And as they develop these new perspectives on simplicity and intention, students may better approach close reading and data analysis having learned that what appears very basic and straightforward is often much more complicated than we realize.

APPLICATION

Social Studies Transform the trajectory of a famous speech into shapes, lines, and colors (this is especially effective while listening to an audio clip of the speech). Use this method to relate the story of a historical person's life or of a significant event. Explain geographical concepts using this strategy.

ELA Translate a poem into a shape story, carefully matching the themes and imagery to relevant colors and geometric figures.

Visual and Performing Arts Record perception of a piece of music while listening to it for the first time, thoughtfully choosing simple metaphorical representations for the instruments, tune progression, and the feelings it conveys. Use geometric shapes and lines to create a short film based on an original screenplay. Study Mondrian's work and the ***De Stijl*** movement to a greater extent and then remix other works of art into his style. Translate a piece of theatre or develop set design using this minimalistic approach.

 AMPLIFICATION

- Use this strategy as a daily reflection, drawing one scene to represent each day. Alternatively, reflect on the quarter, semester, or year.
- Create children's books to inform or inspire, and read them to younger students. Older students may also partner up with younger students and create stop-motion animations based on original stories.
- Start a YouTube channel comprised of student Mondrian-esque video productions sharing lessons of academic value.
- Using social media, work with one or more other schools to create a collaborative story, with each school participating as a designated color and shape. The story can volley back and forth with each party adding something until it is complete.
- If translating a well-known piece of literature, theatre, poetry, or artwork, publicize the Mondrianified work on social media with a challenge to see who can identify it.

ImagED

#IntentionImagED

60 minutes

TARGET

Use images as the sole way to explain a complex concept or as a prompt to elaborate further.

ImagED gives students the opportunity to hone their visual communication skills. They must either distill a complex concept solely into images that convey its essence, or they may use a set of images as a prompt for further elaboration. We highlight three exercises: Icon Challenge, Five-Card Flickr, and Two Images, One Question. You may wish to introduce all three strategies to students and ask them to choose their preference, or you may focus on one strategy depending on the needs of your curriculum.

PATHWAY

Icon Challenge

1. Introduce the concept of "iconography," or "pictograms" (so as not to be confused with the "iconography" as a branch of art history and analysis). Students can share their favorite app icons, for example. Ask them to discuss why they think the icon is successful in communicating an idea in a simple way. If you use something like G Suite for Education, students can drop screenshots of icons into a shared folder for the class to review as a whole.

   Alternatively: Allow students to roam about the campus for a designated time (ten minutes should be sufficient) and use mobile devices to take photos of iconography around the school (restroom signs, recycling icons, etc.). Upon their return, ask them to share their findings and discuss as a class.

2. As students generate their ideas about the nature of icons, they should realize that **simplicity of design** and a certain degree of **universality** is paramount, as icons serve

as symbols, easily interpreted by the eye and brain, representing grander concepts. Shapes, colors, and of course, minimalist pictures play a part in the symbolism, though interpretation may slightly differ from culture to culture. Usually one icon is reductive and conveys a single idea, but combined with other icons, may evolve into something more complex or even a story. Icons are an important part of communication, particularly with digital media, smaller devices, and our increased need to quickly scan. They may also serve as mnemonic devices or visual "memes."

3. Ask students to get into pairs. Distribute **index cards (about six each)**. Present the challenge that they are to each think about their previous day and choose four to six events they participated in (such as brushing teeth, doing homework, etc.). Each student should **draw a simple icon sketch**—one on each card per event. Give students only three minutes to sketch before they must show their partner, in the form of a sequential story of their day. The object is for the partner to guess the activity. Once completed, ask students to discuss what went well and what was misinterpreted, if anything. What elements of their icons were successful, and what could they have designed better?

4. Challenge students to apply the "iconification" idea to a concept they are learning about in class. You might provide a list for them to choose from or allow them to choose from a range (such as something in the unit or chapter). They might choose the life of Marie Antoinette, for example, or the process of cross-pollination. Reiterate that while placed selectively together, **the collection of icons tells a story**. You may designate **how many icons** a student must use, but three to six is optimal.

5. Students should design their own icons, either by hand-drawing or using digital tools. They may use something like thenounproject.com for inspiration. (This is a wonderful site to use during the introductory discussion as well.)

6. Of course, students should **explain their intention**—why they chose those particular aspects of the subject to translate into icons and why they designed the icons as they did.

Five-Card Flickr

The Five-Card Flickr web app (5card.cogdogblog.com) is the brainchild of our friend Alan Levine. A randomizer pulls tagged photos from Flickr into a collection one might use as a story prompt. The serendipitous nature of this visual thinking game makes it fun (and addictive), and the creative constraint of five panels of images inspires the writer who might otherwise be stuck staring at a blank page.

You can use the website as is or **remix it** in the following ways:

Flip It: Instead of writing a story or poem as a response to the image prompt, use an existing poem, text, speech, or even concept (historical event, sport, scientific phenomenon) as the starting point. Then students should take photos, find Creative Commons images online, or even draw images to match "story" of the content. The key is proper synthesis into a finite number of visuals.

Exchange It: Students can collect or create a set of five images, exchange with a peer, and ask the peer to develop the story. This works well for a writing course, but students in other disciplines could be given the constraint of relating the story to the specific course content.

Crowdsource It: If your students have photos on their devices, ask each to choose one or two of their favorites and drop into a shared folder. This collection becomes a sort of private Flickr for students to use in their storytelling.

As with the ***Icon Challenge***, the objective is to get students thinking deeply about what they have learned or investigated and encourage them to share their knowledge visually, tapping into the "essentials" of the content.

Two Images, One Question

This exercise lends itself well to oral presentations of research. Once a student has conducted research on a particular topic, he is asked to "essentialize" it into a slide deck comprised of only two images and one discussion prompt (total of three slides).

Students choose or are assigned a research topic. This works well if there is a general theme, such as "the brain," and students can explore articles and videos about more specific aspects that interest them, such as "psychopathy," "addiction," or "learning." That way, there is variety and novelty in the presentations and subsequent discussions, and students feel they are subject experts and responsible for co-teaching their peers.

After students conduct their research, they should think about the main points they want to relate to the class. Using these notes, they should ***think metaphorically*** about the concepts. While it is tempting to find a more literal visual depiction, remind students that metaphors will be more interesting and more "sticky" in the audience's imagination. To decide upon a metaphorical image, students might want to generate a list of analogies using the question, ***"What is (this concept) like?"*** They should think about common things, such as things in the natural or everyday physical environment, processes that happen daily, or systems they encounter often.

The images students find should serve as prompts for their presentation of the information. They might think of them as points in a narrative, or guideposts on a path. They should strive to **find Creative Commons images** or **create the images themselves** with digital or analog art tools or photography. Some students might go so far as to develop short video clips, such as animated GIFs.

The final of the three slides highlights an original question the students have generated. This question should be open-ended and a bit controversial, because the goal is to spark a class discussion about the topic at hand. Students might need some guidance in this. Remind students that the answers will be less factual and more about feelings, beliefs, speculation, ideas, and opinion. Some helpful starters include:

to what extent . . . ?

how . . . ?

what if . . . ?

why do you think . . . ?

what do you think . . . ?

how do you feel about . . . ?

Research, construction, and presentation times may vary, but allow each students to guide their peers in a short discussion of the prompt. Students should also articulate their creative reasoning behind their choice of images, and if they keep a notebook or blog portfolio, they may include their ideation notes.

TAKEAWAY

By synthesizing complex ideas into simple but poignant images, students demonstrate their personal grasp of the content at hand. Through their choice of what to depict as an image, they assert their individual takeaways from the learning (***metacognition***). The process of selecting appropriate imagery allows them to refine their capacity for ***visual thinking*** and communication, a crucial skill in the new media landscape (***media literacy***). Using images as prompts for storytelling or to frame a narrative in an oral presentation encourages imagination and originality and forces students to break from a copy/paste and bullet-point mentality. Crafting open-ended questions and thinking about ***metaphorical*** representation of an idea demands that students ***think critically.***

APPLICATION

Social Studies Create a biography of a significant individual in history or identify the highlights in a historical event. Or, choose a series of icons that depicts a political or socio-economic philosophy.

World Languages Using the Five-Card Flickr exercise, write a story or poem in the target language. Or use source material to create a series of five images and present the story orally (as a video blog or live).

Health and Physical Education Explain the latest research on an aspect of nutrition or exercise using the Two Images, One Question format.

AMPLIFICATION

- Create a library catalogue of "four-icon novels." Display as posters around campus.
- Use student-designed icon sets to create flashcards for studying.
- Tweet stories using the icon challenges and encourage followers to guess the concept.
- Explore museum sites for images and use in a way similar to Five-Card Flickr.
- ***Four-Square Song:*** Depict a song (or book title, or event) in four images. Check out this Instagram for inspiration: plus.google.com/+AmyBurvall/posts/WYiET7RMUpn. This is really fun if done as a game.

- **Pechaflickr:** Use another Alan Levine creation, pechaflickr.net, to practice World Language skills. (A random slide show is generated based on a designated tag and students must give an impromptu oral presentation with as much confidence as possible.)
- ***Three of Me:*** Choose a (preferably metaphorical) image to show where you've been or where you've come from/where you are now/where you are headed. Feel free to use a collage tool if you have one (or simply hand-draw). This is wonderful as an icebreaker at the beginning of a course or as a reflection at the close of the year.
- ***Say it in Three:*** Take about ten minutes to sketch a storyboard of a process or concept (use something from your discipline) in only three images. You can write a bit of text if you like.
- ***Synthesize Your Day:*** This is a wonderful **reflective tool or exit ticket.** Synthesize your day into one word (drawn with metaphorical typography), three images, a color palette, a few icons or emoji, two photos showing a dichotomy, or something to that effect.

Emoji Story

#IntentionEmoji

60 minutes

TARGET

Tell a story using only emojis.

Emoji Story asks students to retell a complete story—identifying protagonist and antagonist, conflict, rising action, climax, and falling action—using only simple visuals in the form of emojis. It requires students to use visual forms of communication to effectively convey meaning to an audience.

PATHWAY

1. Draw a smiley face on left side of the board and draw a frowny face on the right side of the board.
2. Ask students, "What might happen for a character to go from this (point to smiley face) to this (point to frowny face)?" Solicit suggestions and choose one that is relatively simple, e.g., loses a wallet or gets hurt playing a sport.
3. Write the suggestion in the space between the smiley face and the frowny face, and then ask the class, "How might we show this in one, two, or three very simple doodles?" e.g., a square, a dollar sign, and a question mark, a baseball, and a band aid.
4. Two minutes. Come up with as many simple doodles as you can that tell that story.
5. Share some of the solutions on the board. Challenge students to simplify their doodles as much as possible.
6. Explain to students that this is also how comic strips work. We don't have to see everything that happens to know what is happening from one panel to the next. If we erased the lines (gutters) between each panel, we would still know what is happening.
7. Distribute three very short stories and ask students to read each of them to themselves, noting the characters, the conflicts, the rising action, the climax, and the falling action.

8. Challenge students to retell one of the stories using just the emojis available, putting those emojis into a text message or a Google Doc.

9. Conduct a gallery walk of the emoji stories, asking students to identify the story they believe on display and to conduct a think-aloud, explaining their thinking based on the emojis present.

TAKEAWAY

Emoji Story pushes students to use visual storytelling to take the place of traditional text. It requires them to distill a narrative down to its core elements and represent those elements in a simple, yet detailed way. If there are too few images, the story will be incomplete. If there are too many, the story becomes muddied and difficult to follow.

APPLICATION

Science Explain the process of photosynthesis, the theory of evolution, or the story of inventing human flight.

Social Studies Depict a major battle of the Civil War, an immigrant's experience, or the process of a bill becoming a law.

Visual and Performing Arts Capture the narrative of an opera, retell one act of a Shakespearean play, or choreograph a dance in emoji.

AMPLIFICATION

- Design original content-specific emoji sets and use them in lab reports, reading comprehension checks, and peer-editing sessions.
- Conduct visual class discussions using only emojis on social media.

Haikonography

#IntentionHaiku

45 minutes

TARGET

Compose a visual haiku using only iconography.

Haikonography asks students to apply poetic devices such as repetition, rhyme scheme, figurative language, and diction to the creation of haiku using only visual icons. Students must learn how to convey meaning within structural limitations and through visual communication.

PATHWAY

1. Display a number of frequently seen icons: bathroom signage, railroad crossings, email buttons, and Internet signals. Ask students to identify them.
2. Distribute several examples of haiku and review their essential qualities:

    Present tense
    Seasonal language (kigo)
    Three lines of 5/7/5
    Simple and direct

3. Direct students to thenounproject.com, a community of graphic designers who share their collections of original iconography. Provide a few minutes for them to explore.
4. Challenge students to write a visual haiku using only icons and following these creative constraints:

    Three lines of five icons / seven icons / five icons

    Incorporate at least one seasonal icon (kigo)

    Simple and direct

5. If students struggle with crafting the poem, encourage them to first write the haiku and then translate it into icons.
6. Once students complete their visual haikus, they should write or record a translation to demonstrate their intentions.

7. Conduct a gallery walk or showcase of the haikonography, including student critiques and explanations of intentions.

 TAKEAWAY

Haikonography challenges students to apply visual thinking to a traditionally written medium, giving them the opportunity to practice different forms of communication. The layers of creative constraints require strategic planning, and the creation of a unique medium allows students to act as innovators.

 APPLICATION

Science Craft verse related to the periodic table of elements, chemical bonds, and atomic structures.

Social Studies Design poems illustrating the Great Depression, comparing world religions, and commemorating significant events in local history.

Health and Physical Education Compose haikonography that describes the social groups in the school, expresses understanding of digital citizenship, and conveys knowledge of healthy eating habits.

 AMPLIFICATION

- Use Google Drawing or other graphic design software to create unique icons for haikonography.
- Translate famous haiku from Basho, Issa, and Buson into haikonography.
- Put haikonography on display in the school, accompanied by a marker board or an easel where other students can try their hand at translations.

GIVE ME A LAUNDRY LIST AND I'LL SET IT TO MUSIC

GIOACHINO ROSSINI

CATALOG OF CRITICAL CREATIVITY:

CREATING WITH SOUNDS

Parody Lyrics

Audio Landscape

Q-Llisions

Playlist a Life

Score the News

Song Catching

Soundtracking the Moment

Parody Lyrics

TARGET

Compose parody lyrics to demonstrate understanding of a key concept, historical event, or significant individual while poking fun at both the well-known song and the content itself.

Delivering effective parody lyrics requires students to integrate essential content knowledge and comprehension while applying language devices, such as puns, allusions, juxtaposition, irony, and rhyme scheme.

PATHWAY

1. Ask students if they have ever watched ***Schoolhouse Rock*** or ***Sesame Street***. These television productions often feature parody songs for learning. A popular, recognizable song is reworked with educational lyrics and, in the case of ***Sesame Street***, often performed by the original artist! There are numerous parody music videos uploaded to YouTube, though most are not education-based. Ask students to share examples if they know of them, or explore Amy's own ***History for Music Lovers*** channel for World History and literature-related songs (youtube.com/user/historyteachers).

2. As several examples are shared, ask students what commonalities they see. Some answers could be that ***the songs chosen are well-known***—either popular at the moment, thus tapping into the zeitgeist, or classic hits that resonate with a multigenerational demographic. Students might notice that ***main lyrics often sound like the words in the original***, either by rhyme or assonance. Rhyme, as well as music, ***appeals to memory*** and is therefore a useful strategy in relaying information. Note that parodies are most ***often quite humorous***, but remind students that humor makes things "sticky," so it can be leveraged to facilitate learning. Most

importantly, bring attention to the fact that the best parodies are ***truly transformational***—that is, they reference the original source material but change as much as possible. In fact, part of the Fair Use criteria relates to what extent the new work has transformed and given new meaning to the original. Often what makes parodies strikingly funny is the juxtaposition of two disparate things. When students decide on source material, encourage them to avoid the obvious. For example, if they want to write a song about the Berlin Wall, they should steer clear of Pink Floyd's ***The Wall***.

3. Discuss relevant topic choices with students. They should choose something from the content area that they are intrigued by, and you might find it helpful to provide a list of ideas to spark their thinking. This challenge can either be a demonstration of existing knowledge or learning based on research. If students will need to research, be sure to provide adequate time for them to do so.

4. Set the parameters as to how many facts or allusions to information should be present in the final lyrics. Remind students this is a form of succinct storytelling, and they can play with mixing modern colloquialisms into their lyrics as long as what they are sharing is accurate. You might want to involve students in the process of deciding the criteria as well as analyze some existing parody videos to see how they match.

5. Students should spend some time jotting down vocabulary and phrases that will serve to articulate their knowledge about the topic. As they go, they can make connections and link things that may rhyme. One idea is to write each item on a sticky note or index card and then match them up in a more physical way.

6. Choosing an existing song as source material can happen either before the content ideation or after. Sometimes, the title or main hook line of a song is reminiscent of the subject about which the student is crafting lyrics. A student may also choose the song based on the ***sound of the music*** itself—a fast-paced, accelerating tempo to describe a battle, for example, or a melancholy tune that would match a similar literary character.

7. After the source song is chosen, the student should create a document with two columns and copy the original lyrics to one side of the

page. At this point, it is imperative that the student understands how many syllables are in each line and what the rhyme scheme is. They might want to label numbers for syllables and letters for rhyme scheme on the side of the page. Their new lyrics should attempt to match the original syllabication and rhyme scheme for the best effect.

8. Remind students that iteration is a natural part of the lyric-writing process. They should feel at ease to play with different words and phrasing. They may use an online rhyming dictionary, such as rhymezone.com, to help generate ideas. If students are working independently, you might want to build in a peer-editing process so they get some feedback before recording.

9. After the lyrics are penned, you can stop and ask students to perform ***a capella*** (especially if they have written a rap), or you can pursue the project further with a recording and/or music video. This is highly recommended if you have the time and resources as it engages students in thinking more deeply about the topic, and they can include elements that had to be left out due to the constraints of the lyric scheme.

10. Students can record their song in a variety of ways. Some might be musicians and can use their own instruments with a quality microphone. Others may find an instrumental version of the original song and purchase or download it in order to lay over a vocal track. This is a good chance for them to practice some digital skills if they have not had much practice. Encourage the tech integration specialist to assist, as well as students to work together if possible.

11. Once students have recorded their remix song with the software of their choice, they can plan their music video. They may spend some time free thinking of ideas for how they want the video to look, given the constraints of budget, resources, technical capabilities, and time. Next, they should progress to a storyboard template to plot out how each film frame will look for each line of lyric. The best music videos are fast-paced with different camera angles, multiple costumes, and varied scenery. One can accomplish this even with limited resources (such as one camera). Simply film a few versions of the entire song performance and splice it together in video-editing software. This can even be achieved using a smartphone as a camera. When planning the video, students

should review existing videos (perhaps even the one made for the original song) and identify components to emulate.

12. Challenge students to remain as true to their topic as possible when creating the video concept. Moreover, they can add elements that provide more information for the viewer (things like signage, costumes, props, pantomime, etc.).

13. When students complete their parody music video, celebrate by hosting a film festival. The class can develop both serious and humorous criteria for awards and vote for the winners. Some ideas are: ***"Most True-to-the-Original Song," "Most Informative," "Most Elaborate Production Quality," "Catchiest Lyrics,"*** etc.

TAKEAWAY

Comedy exists at the intersection of the ridiculous and the profound. No matter how silly or foolish, humor that strikes a lasting chord comes from an understanding of the facts and truth. Parody lyrics challenge students to use their factual knowledge in the service of laughter. Students experience how complex, dynamic, and intelligent wit can be, evaluating the effectiveness of their own comedy while strengthening their content understanding.

APPLICATION

Social Studies Tell the story of a historical event or create a biographical song about an important figure. Paraphrase a speech or document to music. Describe a philosophy or movement and its tenets through the lyrics.

ELA Summarize a Shakespearean play or novel into lyrics. Write lyrics in the first person and from the perspective of a literary character. Use a biographical approach to tell the life story of an author or poet, emphasizing his or her creative process. Mix various lines from the poetry of one author or vignettes from several stories of a particular author to create a mashup song.

Science Describe a scientific process with a song. Use a biographical approach to tell the life story of a famous scientist and his or her research or discovery. Use lyrics to remember a concept or collection of facts, such as the periodic table or the domains and kingdoms in biology.

AMPLIFICATION

- As an alternative to video, students may record their voice reciting a poem or singing original song/rap lyrics and upload to soundcloud.com. That link can then be used as annotation on a single image in the thinglink.com app. Or students can use the vocal track with a slide deck and export to Quicktime or another movie file.
- Students can work with peers from another school by composing the lyrics together using digital collaboration tools. Then each school produces a distinct music video. Students can then analyze the interpretations of the lyrics.
- Older students may create lyrics and/or videos to teach younger students. They can either use the content they are studying (if it can be made relevant for younger students) or draw from the content of the lower grade. If they create videos, students from both grade levels can act in the production.
- Start a YouTube channel for your class. Organize the videos into thematic playlists and amplify student work on social media. The authentic feedback they will receive will be worth it.
- Using the suggestion of the video award, create a more elaborate event and invite parents or other classes to attend. Then present the awards at the close. If any students are musicians and can perform the songs live, encourage them to do so (this could work on campus as a "busking" style of activity).

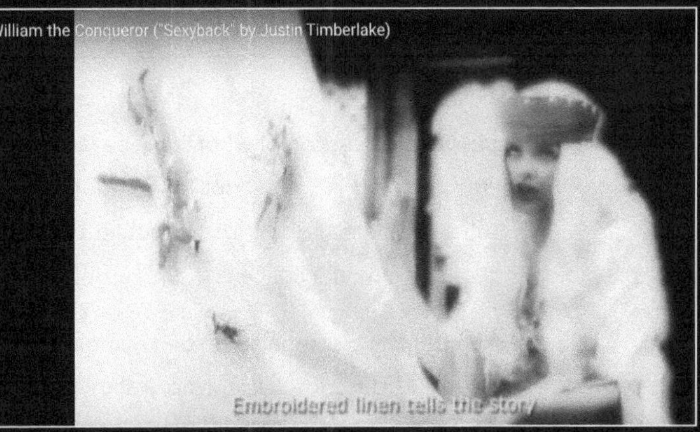

"History for Music Lovers" on YouTube:
youtube.com/user/historyteachers

Audio Landscape

#IntentionAudio

60 minutes

TARGET

Record a collection of obvious and subtle sounds in a given setting to capture the experience of being there for an audience.

Audio Landscape requires students to show their knowledge of a setting or geographic location's defining features through field recordings.

PATHWAY

1. Show students a series of panoramic landscape photographs, both contemporary and classic, including those by Ansel Adams, David Muench, and perhaps even clips from John Ford's ***Rio Grande*** or David Lean's ***Lawrence of Arabia***.

2. Facilitate a discussion of what they see in those images, being as descriptive as possible. Challenge them to look for the subtle details that others may not notice.

3. Ask students to close their eyes and explain how they would describe this setting if they could hear it but not see it. List the sounds they might hear in those spaces. Discuss how different senses can help us notice different features in a setting, and ask them to focus on sounds.

4. Make a list of the sounds students might hear in this classroom. Expand that list with the sounds that would help define this classroom as being unique from any other.

5. Using handheld devices, such as mobile phones or voice recorders, capture the sounds of the room. Encourage students to work in teams and seek out the more unique sounds present. Be careful not to invent sounds—sounds that one wouldn't naturally hear in the room.

6. Send teams of students to various locations around the school—the gym, cafeteria, front lawn, library, main office, etc. Keep the locations secret from the various teams.

7. Return with the recordings to the classroom.
8. Distribute index cards, enough so each student has many index cards as there are settings. Ask students to label "Side A" and "Side B."
9. Conduct a Think-Pair-Share.
    - Three minutes. "Listen to this recording. Fill 'Side A' with notes, jots, and doodles of what you are hearing."
    - Three minutes. "Write a detailed description of the setting you are hearing."
    - Students pair with their partners and share their writings.
    - As ideas are shared, students may add further to their own index cards.
    - Select one or two sentences to share out with the rest of the class.
10. Challenge students to edit their field recordings and create a sonic experience where the sounds arrive in an intentional order, telling a story, and/or capturing a picture in sound.
11. Conduct a listening party for those new recordings where students share their intentions and purpose behind the order of their recordings, including a written piece of documentation with timestamps and identification of each sound.

TAKEAWAY

Audio Landscape is as much an exercise in curation as in creation. Students must discover and record. They must then evaluate the found sounds that best capture what it means to be in that space. The order in which they are delivered and shared matters as much as sounds themselves. They also must listen with intention and seek the details that others may overlook while capturing only the truth of the moment. It can be tempting to create a sound that doesn't normally occur in the name of being clever and/or hilarious.

APPLICATION

Science Select a local ecosystem and capture its details in only sound. Bring those audio landscapes to class and see if the rest of the students can identify where it was recorded.

Social Studies Act as an audio anthropologist and capture the sounds of a local community culture. Consider going to places where people eat, do business, gather, and/or worship.

Visual and Performing Arts Record the sounds of creating a piece of art, i.e., the sound of pencil to paper or paint brush to canvas, clay on the wheel, or chisel into wood. Discuss what the sounds at each stage in the process tell you about the medium and how that can inform your creating.

AMPLIFICATION

- Collaborate with a local broadcast or film-production company to acquire a long-range microphone and see what sounds can be recorded from a distance and not close up.
- Create online sound collages of the community, focusing on a particular theme or type of sound, comparing and contrasting the different ways that sound surfaces. Create an interactive map on Google Maps or use ThingLink to show the locations of those sounds. Consider this a way of finding common ground in the sound.
- Produce podcasts that deliver play-by-plays of these audio landscapes, including the insights students gathered while recording and the details of the spaces they did not notice before.

Q-Llisions

#IntentionQLlisions

30 minutes

TARGET

Produce a video of multiple interviewees answering the same question, using effective editing and storytelling techniques to visualize the process of thinking and illustrating the power of point of view.

Q-Llisions asks students to consider the perspectives and opinions a given population may share regarding a philosophical, ethical, moral, artistic, or personal question. Students must apply visual skills of juxtaposition and sequencing in order to create tension and interest for the viewer, while also demonstrating an understanding of the interviewees' positions and tones.

PATHWAY

1. If possible, watch an episode of "Fifty People, One Question" (fiftypeopleonequestion.com). Point out to students the manner in which the episodes are edited. For example, the question is not revealed until the camera shows several people in "thinking mode." After the reveal, several subjects repeat the question then move on to share more light-hearted answers. The deep, somber, or poignant responses are usually saved until the end, as the music shifts to correspond to the tone.

2. If this is a ***teacher-produced video*** comprised of student responses, tell students you will film them answering the question prompt. Decide on an open-ended prompt that is meaningful to your content. They should say the first answer that comes to mind and not worry about perfection; rather, focus on authenticity and spontaneity. Use a video-recording tool (such as a tablet, smartphone, or digital camera) to capture the footage and a movie-making tool to edit with quick cuts and relevant ambient music. When Amy's students were studying Language as a Way of Knowing in their Theory of Knowledge Course, she asked them to identify the word they think is most beautiful to

the ear, the "ugliest"-sounding word, and the word that in their opinion is the most powerful.

3. If you would like ***students to produce their own video***, discuss possible prompts and help students ideate what question would be intriguing and relevant. They then need to decide who their subjects will be and organize the timing of their filming. Remind them to brief their subjects prior to shooting the footage and that the magic is in the editing. Edits should be quick cutaways and a music track that enhances the message.

4. If you would like to do a ***"VoxBox"***—or self-service video-production system—set up a mounted device, such as a tablet, attached to the wall with industrial-strength Velcro. Post the question prompt(s) and instructions next to it for participants to simply "hit record" in the camera app. These excerpts can later be spliced together in a cohesive mix. You can set a ***VoxBox*** up as a permanent feature of your classroom, perhaps by creating a "niche" space that allows for some privacy and ensures a clean recording of sound. Prompts could be weekly, by thematic unit, or even in response to current events. Perhaps encourage students to provide their own ideas for prompts throughout the year and take charge of the compilation video editing.

TAKEAWAY

By creating a supercut of these interviews, Q-Llisions challenges students to unpack the points of view of many individuals and look for the threads that unite them, while also looking for the moments of dissent. It also requires a deeper look at visible thinking routines and processes, as students must also integrate footage of the respondents thinking, considering, and working their ways through the answers. Rather than just an exercise in video editing, it challenges students to tell the story of answering a question—and the various ways in which a question might be answered—through the use of image, sound, and content. They discover the nuances of answering questions while working with the essentials of telling another's story.

APPLICATION

Social Studies and History Students can vlog from a specific point of view as they assume the role of a character and respond to a question (for example, a Patriot versus a Loyalist in the American Revolution). Students studying a particular poem, speech, or document (like the ***Bill of Rights***) could each film themselves reading a bit of it. Psychology course prompts could relate to behavior or emotion—two general topics which lend themselves readily to open-ended, diverse responses. Current events are often controversial and encourage a diversity of thoughtful, open-ended responses. Give students the guideline that they should defend their position with examples and describe their path of reasoning.

World Languages Vlogging is a natural fit for language study. Pose the prompt in the target language and students can practice responding in a conversational tone. Specific vocabulary terms can be used as a creative constraint—provide a short list of apropos terms and challenge students to include one or more in their recording.

Arts Prompts could be visual, such as a photograph or image of a two- or three-dimensional piece of art. Participants could be asked to provide one word or phrase as their gut reaction to the piece or to describe the emotion the work conveys. Alternatively, interviewees could be challenged to develop a question they have concerning the work of art.

Mathematics Prompts could include, ***In what ways do you use math in your daily life? What is your favorite math formula and why? Describe a scenario where you would use (a particular math equation, theorem, or formula) to solve a real-world problem.***

AMPLIFICATION

- Crowdsource the video responses using social media. Participants can send short video clips you can splice together or respond to by text, and students can record their voices reading the answers. Try the Flipgrid app, which allows you to post a prompt and participants to respond in the grid with short videos."

- Connect with another class from across the globe. One idea is to exchange different prompts. This gives one group of children insight into other perspectives.
- Encourage students to become journalists and develop their own Q-Llision project. They may use their mobile devices to record sound clips as they interview subjects around campus or their local area. They may then produce the final video with simple editing software and an emotive soundtrack.
- Use a VoxBox at a parent night or other event to crowdsource responses from parents or the extended community. VoxBoxes are ideal for capturing reactions at special events, such as drama productions or science fairs.

Playlist a Life

#PlaylistALife #IntentionPlaylist

90 minutes

TARGET

Create a biographical playlist of songs to demonstrate deeper understanding of the life and times of the subject.

Playlist a Life asks students to interpret the life of a subject through a musical lens. Students must identify lyrical, tonal, or thematic connections between music selections and the biographical history of a given subject.

PATHWAY

1. Warm up student thinking by conducting a brief autobiographical activity.

    - Distribute index cards, one per student. Ask students to label "Side A" and "Side B."
    - Three minutes. "Fill 'Side A' with a list of experiences you've had in your life so far that mean something to you. Think about gifts you've received, places you've visited, people you've met, and challenges you've encountered."
    - Three minutes. "Fill 'Side B' with a list of songs that mean something to you. They might be songs you enjoy or songs you connect to certain moments, people, or places in your life."
    - Ask students to try and connect the dots between the experiences on Side A and the songs on Side B.
    - Solicit volunteers to share some of their connections.

2. Provide students three to five individuals with biographies worth investigating. Limiting the number of subjects provides a fantastic opportunity to compare and contrast students' playlist selections and/or conduct a collaborative experience.

3. Ask students to identify three significant moments/achievements in the subjects' lives: perhaps one from childhood (if available), one or two from adolescence/young adult life, and one from adulthood. Provide time for students to research using reliable sources.

4. Present the creative challenge, "How might we represent that individual's life in a music playlist?"

5. Instruct students to find songs to represent these significant moments in the subjects' lives—one song per moment for a grand total of three songs. Suggest students consider lyrical content, musical tone or atmosphere, or overall thematic feel of the songs when making connections.

6. Compile the playlists on digital services, such as YouTube or Spotify.

7. Require students to write or record the intention behind each of their musical choices, checking for depth of connection between the songs and the life experiences.

TAKEAWAY

Playlist a Life challenges students to make connections between seemingly unrelated contexts. Requiring students to conduct biographical research pushes students to think critically about the relationship between an individual's youth experiences and adult achievements. Crafting a playlist based on these understandings demands students take a deeper look at the music they know and apply it to solving a problem.

APPLICATION

Science Research important figures from the study of astronomy, biology, or physics, and put their lives to music.

Social Studies Investigate political revolutionaries of the twentieth century, religious leaders of the nineteenth century, or military leaders of the eighteenth century, and capture their lives in song.

ELA Uncover the lives of Beat poets, Native American writers, or expatriate novelists, and share their experiences through lyrics and sound.

AMPLIFICATION

- Design and publish biographical websites using a free tool, such as Google Sites, Weebly, or Wix, and embed the playlists alongside researched information and images.
- Create "Music by Which to Study" playlists as exam review.
- Write an original composition inspired by one or more of the songs on the playlist that tells the biographical story of the subject.

Score the News

#IntentionScoring

45 minutes

TARGET

Compose music to accompany a broadcast news story.

Score the News asks students to identify the factual information of a news story and use original music to relate the underlying importance or impact of that news to an audience.

PATHWAY

1. Play students a recent news story from NPR's ***Morning Edition*** or ***All Things Considered*** that is followed by a musical interlude. These are often found between the top and bottom of the hour, usually around the fifteen-minute mark.

2. Facilitate an investigation into the news story.

   - Work as a class to identify the journalistic five Ws of the story by putting up two columns on the board: Information and Impact.
   - Who is involved in these events? Who is impacted by this information?
   - Where did the events take place? Where will the impact of this information be felt?
   - When did the events take place? When is this information going to have an impact?
   - What actually happened? What will be the impact as a result of this?
   - Why did these events happen? Why will it have an impact on others?

3. Explore the musical interlude that followed the news story as a class.

   - Brainstorm a list of adjectives to describe the music.
   - Follow this brainstorm with a list of adjectives that absolutely ***do not*** describe the music. (Determining a false answer can

often be just what a student needs to help find the words to capture a truth.)

4. Ask students to map the adjectives that describe the music to the information from the articles. "Let's link the descriptions to the events and impact of these events."

5. Discuss why the music supervisor/producer chose this particular selection to accompany the story.

6. Pose the creative challenge. "Now it is your turn to create a piece of original music to accompany a broadcast news story to demonstrate your understanding of the facts and the impact of that news."

7. Provide students three recent broadcast news pieces from either news radio or television/cable media. Choose one of local, one of national, and one of global relevance. For time management purposes, look for pieces around three minutes in length.

   - Direct students toward free web-based tools, such as SoundTrap and BeatsLab, to compose their original works. Encourage them to use their own instruments or a capella skills as well.

   - Provide students twenty minutes to unleash their inner Bernsteins, their hidden Williamses, their latent Zimmers, and their potential Mancinis.

   - Conduct a showcase where students share their compositions and explain their intentions between their creations and the information and impact of the news piece.

TAKEAWAY

Score the News challenges students to find the connections between information and emotion and experience the value music brings to context and meaning. Composing original music for its own sake is one thing; to do so in the service of enhancing information and an audience's experience requires students to practice deeper empathy.

APPLICATION

Science Seek news stories related to developments in plate tectonics, endangered species, and space exploration, while requiring students to incorporate sounds that mimic those of the natural and astronomical subjects of the articles.

World Languages After finding stories related to a particular country or region, ask students to incorporate music styles and instrumentation associated with that particular culture.

Mathematics Using stories related to the application of math to problem-solving contexts, challenge students to create music compositions that follow a particular curve trajectory in terms of complexity, volume, or intensity, that function as palindromes, or that illustrate addition, subtraction, or multiplication properties.

AMPLIFICATION

- Publish student compositions online and deliver them to the original news agency for critique and feedback.
- Collaborate with the music program to compose original works based on a thematic collection of news stories to be performed by school musical ensembles. Stage a public performance with the pieces played, while the audience watches the original pieces on mobile devices or projected in the venue.
- Remix student compositions on collaborative music tools such as BeatLabs or using HitRecord.org.
- Research the professional world of musical scoring by listening to podcasts such as Edmund Stone's ***The Score*** or WNYC's ***RadioLab***, and apply one of the techniques discovered.

Song Catching

#IntentionSong

30 minutes

TARGET

Gather a collection of songs by asking people in the class, around the school, or on the streets to perform songs that evoke a particular emotion, concept, or theme.

Song Catching challenges students to illustrate their understanding of an emotion, concept, or theme by relying upon the ideas of others and making connections between those ideas and their own. They must be able to convey that understanding to others to ensure the song's recording suits the purpose.

PATHWAY

1. Three minutes. Ask students to list the last songs they remember singing or being heard sung by a family member, friend, or passerby.

2. Distribute sticky notes and ask students to choose one song from their individual lists and write the title on the note.

3. Work as a class to sort the collection of songs on sticky notes. See what trends emerge. Look for patterns. Ask students to consider the sorts of songs people enjoy singing, tend to sing, and remember singing.

4. After setting those patterns aside, ask them to consider the emotions the protagonists in a particular story have been experiencing, the key elements of a current concept being discussed, or an emerging theme or big idea in the current unit of study.

5. Distribute index cards and instruct students to make concept maps, outlines, or doodles that connect the ideas from the current content learning to one or more of the songs identified on the sticky notes. Explain to the students this is just warm-up thinking; their challenge is greater.

6. Send students "song catching," a term coined by Grateful Dead drummer Mickey Hart, for a field recording of the music of a community or culture.

    - Go around the school and ask people if they are willing to be volunteers for your song-catching project.
    - When someone is willing, ask them to think of a song that reminds them of your emotion, concept, or theme. If they do not have working knowledge of your emotion, concept, or theme, you must explain it to them. Record the song they choose.
    - If you and the volunteer are unable to come up with song idea connecting to the concept or theme within sixty seconds, ask the volunteer to sing any song they like. Make a recording.
    - Return to the room once you have collected three songs or fifteen minutes, whichever comes first.

7. Ask students to review the songs they have collected and justify each song's connection to the concept or theme. This will be especially challenging for those who had to collect a more random assortment of songs, and at the same time, it will be an excellent opportunity to look for connections in seemingly unrelated texts.

8. Share their collections and written or recorded rationales to demonstrate the intentional thinking behind their song catches.

TAKEAWAY

Song Catching layers in two levels of intentionality. Students must understand the concepts and themes well enough to explain them to others and collaborate with individuals who may be unfamiliar with the ideas. Students must then be able to articulate back to their peers how seemingly unrelated ideas connect to a key understanding. They must also practice empathy with their recording subjects, learn to make meaningful asks to other individuals, and honor the vulnerability that comes with public performance.

APPLICATION

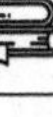

ELA Collect songs to relate to the protagonist of a novel, the speaker of poem, or the feelings one associates with the writing process.

Social Studies Collect songs that relate to revolution, democracy, and citizenship. Song catch in order to determine what songs are most culturally relevant to the school and/or local community.

Mathematics Catch songs that relate to mathematical properties, geometric principles, or statistical analysis.

AMPLIFICATION

- Open class with an improv game called "Musical Hot Spot." Form a circle. One person steps into the middle, starts singing a song, and the rest of the group joins. Other players listen for inspiration. When a new player thinks of a song related to the first in some way, the middle player is tapped out and the new song begins. Tap the player in the middle to take his or her place, and begin singing a new song that is somehow connected to the first. For example, the first song might be Taylor Swift's "Shake It Off," which transitions into Outkast's "Hey Ya!", which turns to Ed Sheeran's "Photograph," and so on.
- Investigate patterns that emerge throughout the song-catching collections. Use those patterns to formulate hypotheses or position statements regarding attitudes toward a particular concept or feeling.
- Challenge students to go out and catch songs prior to any discussion of concepts or themes. Make the connections between the random songs caught and the content.
- Put a twist on Song Catching by recording any music you hear or discover people listening to as well. Take note of the extent to which people are able to sing the music they hear.

Soundtracking the Moment

#SoundtrackingtheMoment
#IntentionSoundtrack
30 minutes

TARGET

Create an alternative soundtrack for a film clip that transforms the tone, mood, or atmosphere of the film.

Soundtracking the Moment asks students to identify the tone, mood, or atmosphere of a particular film and then modify the audience's experience by choosing a different song to accompany the film.

PATHWAY

1. Access YouTube channels, such as Movie Clips or websites such as WingClips, to access categorized lists of film clips.

2. Show students a brief film clip on mute and ask them to take note of the action in the scene and the emotions the characters seem to be conveying. The helicopter attack from ***Apocalypse Now***, the boombox scene from ***Say Anything***, and the slow clap from ***Rudy*** all work well for this activity.

3. Play a series of songs to accompany the clips. Choose one that aligns well to the original intention of the clip, one that seems completely misaligned in an almost ridiculous way, and one that transforms the original intention of the clip in an interesting, unique, or meaningful way. For example, when using the clip from ***Say Anything***, one might use Peter Gabriel's "In Your Eyes" (the original song used), Sir Mix-a-Lot's "Baby Got Back" for an absurd response, and Johnny Cash's cover of Nine Inch Nails' "Hurt" to evoke a different feel altogether.

4. Choose three to five clips that have distinctive tones, moods, or atmospheres. Limiting the choices of clips creates an opportunity to compare and contrast different solutions. Sports films, action thrillers, and historical dramas tend to work very well for this activity.

5. Ask students to use any available music collections or digital tools, such as YouTube, Vimeo, or Spotify, to find songs they believe would serve as effective, absurd, and transformative soundtracks for that clip.

6. Instruct students to identify key lyrics and/or timestamp moments where their intentions are evident.

7. Conduct a showcase where students present their choices to the class, share their intentions, and receive feedback. Look for opportunities for students to share various approaches to the same film clip.

TAKEAWAY

Soundtracking the Moment challenges students to consider a creator's original intentions while also finding ways to manipulate the effects music can have on an audience. Requiring students to find anti-examples, songs that do not fit well, is an effective way of demonstrating purpose, especially when students articulate why the choice is such a poor example.

APPLICATION

ELA Change the musical background for a film clip and choose the best tone word to describe the effects. Select a theme and use the music choices to make a series of clips to suit the theme.

Health and Physical Education Select soundtrack clips from inspirational sports films or documentaries about the food industry.

World Languages Use clips from foreign films and replace the subtitles with lyrics from the selected songs.

AMPLIFICATION

- Compile an alternative soundtrack to accompany a feature-length film. Include timestamps for specific placement and rationales for each song choice.
- Produce short films to accompany a particular song. Try creating films that produce different effects when paired with the song.
- Compose original songs to accompany the film clips.
- Use news footage in place of the film clips. (See also ***Score the News,*** page 198.)

IDEAS ARE BORN FROM WHAT IS SMELLED, HEARD, SEEN, EXPERIENCED, FELT, EMOTIONALIZED

ROD SERLING

CATALOG OF CRITICAL CREATIVITY:

CREATING WITH THE BODY

Humojis

Custom Signage

Dallowinian Party

Machine Made

Sensory Map

Tableaux Repreaux

Chronological Choreography

Humojis

#IntentionHumojis

45 minutes

TARGET

Use physical bodies, facial expressions, and digital photography to create a customized set of emoji/emoticons for communicating ideas, expressing reactions, and taking notes. Create an accessible gallery of humojis to use for marking up digital texts, crafting visual narratives, and sharing points of view in silent discussion.

Humojis challenge students to reimagine common iconographic and visual symbols through personalization and physicality. Students analyze their own language and responses for patterns and tendencies, prioritizing and selecting the images worth including in their early vocabulary. They must work within the creative constraints of collaboration, physical body and facial features, digital imagery, and a time limit of only fifteen minutes to create their first lexicon.

PATHWAY

1. Ask students to doodle well-known emojis on an index card. Keep passing the cards around every fifteen seconds until the card is filled with as many hand-drawn versions of emojis as you can muster. Continue for three minutes. Circulate the cards and identify frequently appearing emojis. Share these with the room by doodling on the marker board or describing them.
2. Divide the class into trios—pairs if necessary—and ensure each group has a photo-taking device.
3. Deliver the challenge.
   - "You have fifteen minutes to create a set of ten humojis, human-made emojis. We will be using these humojis to communicate in class as well mark up a text with notes

and reactions, so consider the expressions, doodles, emojis, and symbols the members of your group use most often. Make a set that you know you will be able to use right away."

- "Get into position and document your humojis with your camera. You may rotate roles as well, so one group member does not have to take all of the pics."
- Provide fifteen minutes for students to go and capture their humojis.

4. Organize and share the humojis.
   - "Upload your humojis to Google Drive in a folder. Make sure you name each humoji so that you can remember your intentions and find them quickly."
   - "Share your humoji Google Drive folder with me and all of your group members. I will be making a master folder with every set of humojis in the class so you can use one another's sets."
   - "Be certain to share your humojis with your group members and then upload them into a folder on Google Drive for easy access later. Also, make sure you title each humoji!"
5. Use the humojis to mark up a brief digital text with reactions and responses.
   - "Take a look at the short article I've shared with you as a Google Drawing on Google Drive. It's a Drawing because that will let you use your humoji pictures to add notes right to the text."
   - Read through the article as a class.
   - "Now, use your humojis to mark up the text by inserting the images from your Google Drive and use the 'Arrange' menu to make sure the picture is floating on top of the article where it can be seen. You can also use arrows and lines to make connections from the humoji to the place in the text you want to note."
6. Ask students to compose a reaction or personal response to the text using humojis, accompanied by a written or recorded translation.

TAKEAWAY

Humojis may be replacing tools already at students' disposal, yet the process of creating their own by using their physical bodies engages kinesthetic learners, while also challenging students to consider the design and purpose of effective emojis. Developing the basics of a visual language also requires students to think about how we communicate, how we establish mutual understanding, and the differences and similarities between visual and verbal communication.

APPLICATION

Mathematics Create a series of humojis to represent mathematical operations, functions, or expressions. Use those humojis to provide peer feedback during a practice check, to identify operations necessary toward solving a word problem, or to communicate questions about an assignment.

Social Studies Develop a lexicon of humojis to use with primary-source government documents, such as the Declaration of Independence or the Magna Carta. Mark up digital versions of those texts with those humojis. Translate a portion of those documents into humojis.

Science Design a series of humojis to represent the phase of cellular reproduction, the stages in photosynthesis, or the scientific process. Use the humojis to annotate cell slides, photos of photosynthesis in action, or the narrative of a lab report. Consider developing a humoji periodic table of elements, particularly for the most frequently occurring elements.

AMPLIFICATION

- Build human infographics. If we can represent emojis in human form, why not sets of data as well? Challenge students to arrange themselves to visually represent the ideas in the data set, as well as growth, change, comparisons, and more.

- Develop a complete set of humojis for a variety of contexts and situations. Have students choose interest areas to develop sets of humojis for each including sports, food, entertainment, and academics.

- Collaborate with the special education department to design picture schedules from humojis that your students' peers, as well as younger and older nonverbal students, may use to communicate ideas. Conduct empathy interviews with the students, their educators, and families to determine what might be the most useful words and concepts to include in the vocabulary.

Custom Signage

#IntentionSign
60 minutes

 TARGET

Develop a set of custom hand signs to communicate a process nonverbally.

Custom Signage asks students to define technical, content-specific terms and concepts. While there may be American Sign Language (ASL) gestures for these terms, students must determine unique physical hand figures and movements that convey their understanding to an audience. The custom signs must also be reproduced by others, distinguishing this activity from charades or pantomiming. Students must stay within the creative constraints of silence, physicality, and a time limit.

PATHWAY

1. Stand in front of the class and ask them to interpret several common hand signals or body gestures as you provide them. Try a thumbs-up and a thumbs-down, an okay, an I-don't-know shrug, and a so-so hand wiggle. Explain that these are informal signs but are widely recognized and understood.
2. Share a music video featuring sign-language interpretation of a song. Ask students what they notice about the signs used, common characteristics in the movements, and shapes.
3. Direct students to explore online ASL dictionaries and tutorials, such as SigningSavvy.com and ASLPro.com, looking for words and terms related to their personal interests and curiosities.
4. Ask students to find and practice one sign to share with the class.
5. After sharing, ask students to review any notes or materials they have regarding the current process they are studying.

6. Present the creative challenge: Create a set of custom signs to explain each step, stage, or phase in the process.

7. Pose the creative constraints:

    - Ten minutes to create
    - Must remain silent when making the sign
    - Must keep the movement and gestures above the waist

8. Allow students to work in design teams of two or three to complete the challenge.

9. Provide ten minutes for students to create their custom signs.

10. If devices are available, ask students to document their signs and processes.

11. Pair design teams and ask teams to present and teach their custom signs to one another.

12. After ten minutes, establish another set of pairings. This time, however, teams present the custom signs and processes they just learned from their peers.

13. As each team watches, ask them to translate the custom gestures.

14. Come together as a class and discuss the successes and struggles they experienced with this challenge. Identify the qualities and characteristics of signs that made for effective communication.

TAKEAWAY

Custom Signage requires students to think about communication as a physical and visual experience. Developing unique terms to add to the ASL lexicon presents the opportunity to explore how language develops. Thinking about processes in terms of component parts and phases pushes students to zoom in for a more careful examination.

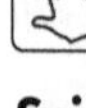

APPLICATION

Science Create language for the oxygen cycle, the scientific process, or nuclear fission.

ELA Articulate the writing process, a close-reading strategy, or how to publish one's work on a blog.

Health and Physical Education Explain how to diaper a baby, how to fry an egg, or how to serve a tennis ball.

AMPLIFICATION

- Design a complete class dictionary of custom signs and publish them online for others to use.
- Compare and contrast students' custom signs to their ASL counterparts. Remix the custom sign processes by infusing ASL language into the explanations.

Dallowinian Party

#IntentionParty

60 minutes

TARGET

Demonstrate the personality traits and mindsets, relationships, and dynamics of a group of individuals or characters by staging an improvised, role-play dinner party. During periodic breaks in the action, use first-person, in-character, stream-of-consciousness journaling to explore the attendees' thoughts and feelings.

Based upon Virginia Woolf's novel, ***Mrs. Dalloway***, Dallowinian Party asks students to look at the hidden motivations of behavior and to understand the why and the reasoning behind the choices and decisions people make. It requires students to understand the backgrounds of the dinner guests, the contexts in which they know the other attendees, and to portray those figures in a manner consistent with the inspirations for those characters. Students must work within the creative constraints of the source material, the expression of ideas through first-person stream of consciousness, and a series of plot twists and interruptions provided by the facilitator.

PATHWAY

1. Prior to the party itself, some preparation is necessary.
    - Create a list of guests ***inspired*** by historical figures or fictional characters. Developing original characters challenges students to apply their knowledge of the source material while giving them freedom to explore their own ideas as well.
    - Determine which of these characters will serve as the host.
    - Provide students time to develop those characters and write brief profiles of those characters including such details as name, age, occupation, religion, and a short biography, as well as a description of their relationship to the host.

- Work as a class to build a map, flowchart, or family tree of sorts, making the extent to which the guests know one another, how they feel about one another, and any history they share.
- Collaborate on a list of "interruptions," plot events, or twists that may occur randomly during the party itself. These might be "reveal a secret," "accuse someone of spreading a lie," "leave the room and discover a dead body," or "confess your love." Put these interruptions on slips of paper and into a bowl for the party.
- Review a simplified version of stream-of-consciousness writing: the act of writing a character's thoughts from a first-person point of view and flowing from idea to idea—whatever is coming to mind for that character in the moment.
- Encourage students to find costume pieces, props, and other items that might heighten the experience during the actual party.

2. On the day of the party itself, arrange the room to host the event, putting desks and chairs around the outside of the space. Students will need to sit in these, so make them available. Lay out food, props, and other furniture for the guests.
3. Send the guests into the hallway, leaving the host in the room. Give instructions for each guest to arrive at one-minute intervals. Provide a means for them to keep track of time if they don't have one.
4. As guests arrive, the host interacts and helps establish the relationship and dynamic between them. The teacher observes and takes note, a fly on the wall.
5. Every five minutes, play a tone or signal for the party to pause. Guests immediately go to the seats around the room and write in first-person stream of consciousness what they are thinking at that moment. Provide three minutes to write.
6. As guests write, discreetly provide the bowl with interruption slips to one of the guests. Ask them to draw a single interruption and apply it during the next scene of the party.

7. After three minutes, start the party once again.
8. Repeat steps 5 through 7 for a number of scenes, each time tightening the length of the scenes and the writing sessions by thirty seconds. The intent is to increase the intensity of the experience as more events occur and guests have more to consider.
9. After the thirty-second scene, end the party.
10. Conduct a debriefing for students to discuss their roles and experiences during the party. Ask them to conduct an analysis of their writings: To what extent did their thoughts and interactions at the party align to the mindset, personality, and experiences of the inspiration source for their character? What might they do differently next time? What might they keep the same?

TAKEAWAY

Dallowinian Party requires students to apply their knowledge of characters and personalities to an interactive and original context. Role-playing these guests challenges students to think about how movement, language, and appearance all contribute to how an individual is perceived by others. The stream-of-consciousness writing and analysis reveals the depth to which the students understand the source material and improve their ability to empathize with others by adopting alternative points of view to their own.

APPLICATION

Science Stage a dinner party featuring famous scientists from different eras, researchers from various areas of study, or advocates with a range of positions on controversial topics.

Social Studies Gather guests from the French Revolution, the Italian Renaissance, or the British Music Invasion.

World Languages Bring together tour guides from around the world, translators from the United Nations, or families from immigrant communities.

AMPLIFICATION

- Film the party from a number of points of view using GoPro cameras or handheld devices. Edit the various points of view into a short video that tells a cohesive narrative about the party. Use stream-of-consciousness writings as voiceover material.
- Evolve the stream-of-consciousness writings into short stories or the basis for a research or position paper.
- Place the bowl of interruptions on the table and allow the guests to decide when to add new wrinkles into the action.

Machine Made

#IntentionMachine

30 minutes

TARGET

Design a machine that solves a problem, using people as the medium out of which the machine will be constructed. Students become the parts and pieces of the machine, applying the improvisational acting skill of mirroring and complementing to create a complete prototype.

Machine Made requires students to analyze a problem for its component parts and develop a prototype solution to that problem. Students must know the features and tensions of the problem, the context in which the problem exists, and consider the users who will experience their solutions. Students must learn to think about movement and resources in flexible ways and must work within the creative constraints of materials and time.

PATHWAY

1. Brainstorm a list of all of the items in the room that are likely machine-made. Include such things as articles of clothing, nuts and bolts, water bottles, etc.

2. Distribute index cards and ask students to doodle the machine they believe made one of those items. "What does a bolt-making machine look like? What does a water bottle-making machine look like? Don't worry about being right or wrong. Use what you know and put that together with your imagination." Model this process by doodling one on the board before the students begin.

3. Provide three minutes to doodle.

4. Conduct a brief Think-Pair-Share to see what ideas students have about these machines.

5. Explain the improv acting skill of mirrors and complements.

   - Ask a volunteer to stand and strike a pose.

- Ask another volunteer to stand and strike that same pose. Explain that this is a mirror: doing the same thing as your partner. Even if facing in a different direction, standing across the room, or laying down, if the pose and position of the body is the same, it is a mirror.
- Ask another volunteer to strike a new pose.
- Now ask for a volunteer to adopt a pose that would go well with the first but not be the same thing. For example, if someone were standing and looking down, a partner might kneel and hold out one's hands as though proposing marriage. Explain that this is a complement: doing something that works together with your partner to make a picture, a scene, or a relationship. It should still be frozen, like a photo of the moment.

6. Brainstorm a new list on the board. Ask students, "What problems have we been learning about lately?"
7. After making the list, work as a class to determine which problem they most want to solve in the next ten minutes.
8. Pose the creative challenge: "How might we build a machine to solve that problem?"
9. Present the creative constraints.
10. The machine must be made out of people. Use mirrors and complements to establish the various parts of the machine.
11. There must be moving parts.
12. Each stage of the machine must have a specific purpose.
13. Work in groups of four, five, or six people. People may move from one stage of the machine to another to represent another part.
14. Ten minutes to create.
15. Provide ten minutes to design and construct the machines.
16. Conduct a showcase for students to share their machines, discuss their intentions, and receive feedback. If time permits, allow students to create second iterations of their machines.

TAKEAWAY

Machine Made asks students to prototype solutions to a problem while remaining within a set of constraints. Students learn to use only the materials available, applying them in unique and creative ways. The time constraints push students to take action and solve the problem by doing rather than waiting. Mirrors and complements require collaboration, and the focus on problem solving demands each choice in the design be intentional.

APPLICATION

Science Create machines that restore the polar ice caps, provide new forms of renewable energy, and deliver mass transit to rural populations.

ELA Construct machines that write haiku, translate Shakespeare, and provide feedback on essays.

Health and Physical Education Design machines that help others in the room deal with their daily struggles, provide a complete upper-, lower-, and cardio-body workout, and turn raw ingredients into a five-course meal.

AMPLIFICATION

- Work together as an entire class to remix a complex machine that incorporates the best features of the groups' machines.
- Use the human prototypes as the first iteration before completing a physical prototype made out of more traditional materials. Present those new prototypes to organizations and companies working on those problems to practice the real-world skills of communicating intentions and pitching ideas to stakeholders.
- Gather volunteers from other classes to come and serve as the raw material for the designs. Provide a form of currency (candy, school-store credits, or hugs), establish a market value, and require design teams to budget for the number of students they will be using.

Sensory Map

#IntentionSenses
90 minutes

TARGET

Map a setting by identifying features that appeal to each of the senses and collecting physical evidence that represents those features.

Students build their Sensory Maps by first examining the setting carefully, drawing on diction or context clues to make conclusions about what sensory details are evident and what might be inferred. They must then find representations of those senses, applying their thinking and evaluating the effectiveness a given texture, smell, sight, sound, or taste might have in conveying this information to someone unfamiliar with that setting. The only creative constraint is nonverbal—students may not label or use words in their evidence, including sights.

PATHWAY

1. Prior to the lesson some preparation is necessary.
    - Gather materials for sensory-evidence collection: zipper-lock bags, tissues, cotton balls, shopping bags, baby-food jars, gloves, shoe boxes, audio-recording devices, cameras, etc.
    - Collect a selection of sensory substitutes: materials that might easily replicate other sensory evidence, i.e., small stones, pieces of flooring, wood, plastic, or baby-food jars with cotton balls featuring a number of fragrances, etc.
2. Ask students to close their eyes and listen to the room. As they hear noises in the room, they should raise their hands. When called upon, they may identify what they heard. Record their responses on the board.
3. Ask students to shift their focus to the smells in the room. Repeat the recording process.

4. Then ask students to open their eyes, circulate the room, seek out interesting textures and touch them. Repeat the recording process.

5. Repeat the above for sight and then discuss how tastes are more difficult. Ask students which sense works most with taste and facilitate a conversation around the relationship between smells and tastes.

6. Distribute three excerpts from short stories and/or articles in which a setting is described using all five senses.

7. Allow the class to break into groups of one, two, or three.

8. Provide time for the groups to familiarize themselves with each of the three readings and ask them to choose the one they find the most interesting, effective, or enjoyable.

9. Distribute paper and ask them to divide the paper into five columns and doodle a symbol to represent each of the five senses at the top of the columns. Tell the students to use each column to note, jot, or doodle evidence from the readings.

10. Pose the creative challenge: Gather evidence from around the school campus to create a sensory map of the setting in your reading. Gather evidence so effective that anyone who experiences your map will be able to describe your setting without having read it.

11. Provide the creative constraint: nonverbal. Students may not label or use words in their evidence, including sights.

12. Offer students materials in the room for collecting their sensory map evidence as well as access to the sensory substitutes.

13. Send students out to collect their evidence, reminding them that tastes may be very difficult and finding two distinct smells may be enough to capture taste. The only tastes gathered should be edible ones.

14. Upon returning, ask group members to determine the order in which someone should interact with their evidence.

15. Pair the groups. Determine a Share Group and an Experience Group.

16. Instruct the Share Group to share their evidence with the members of the Experience Group by guiding them through each sense and allowing time to interact with each piece of evidence in the proper order.
17. Groups then switch roles and repeat that process.
18. Ask students to then work independently to write or record their description of the unfamiliar setting they just encountered through their senses. Encourage them to use sensory image and strong diction.
19. Reform the Share and Experience Group pairs to assess the sensory maps' effectiveness in helping others to experience the settings. Discuss the intentions behind each piece of evidence.

TAKEAWAY

Sensory Map challenges students to consider the relationship between written description and physical reality and to develop a further appreciation for effective prose. It requires students to engage in all of their senses and focus on those that they may often overlook. By creating the sensory map for others, students must evaluate the effectiveness of their evidence as they attempt to communicate through the senses with their intended audience.

APPLICATION

Social Studies Capture the setting of a marketplace in China, a bakery in France, or a seaport in Sweden.

Science Map a marshland, a desert, a coniferous forest, or another biome.

Visual and Performing Arts Design a set for a play, ballet, or opera based on the sensory needs described in the script, the choreography, or the libretto.

AMPLIFICATION

- Craft narratives based on the sensory maps. Publish the narratives online using images and sounds from the sensory maps as illustrations and interactives.
- Conduct sociological and ethnographic research by gathering sensory data from students' homes. Sort the data, look for trends, and develop a cultural profile for the class population. The same could be done for the school.
- Focus on just one sense (see Audio Landscape) and attempt to capture the entirety of a setting based on that one sense alone.
- Investigate synesthesia, a sensory condition which causes some people to hear colors, feel sounds, etc. Explore what it would be like for a synesthete to experience those settings. Employ some empathy and try to develop a sensory map from that point of view.

Tableaux Repreaux

#IntentionTableaux

  30 minutes

TARGET

Create a visual representation of a key historical moment by adopting a freeze—actors standing in character and position without moving. Think of it as taking a picture of a moment in history and recreating that picture through a silent, frozen pantomime.

Tableaux Repreaux requires students to identify context clues and central figures of a historical moment, consider how to arrange the characters, how to portray the emotions, and how to integrate significant objects or setting details. Students must work within the creative constraints of silence and stillness.

PATHWAY

1. Ask students to stand in a circle and then turn to face outward. This provides some comfort for the more introverted students.
2. Take them through a brief acting exercise, "Four Faces," asking them to make a face for each of the four core emotions: fear, joy, sorrow, and anger.
3. After "Faces," ask them to do the same, but this time adding physicality and movement.
4. Direct them to examine the historical moments they are currently studying, taking note of the people, settings, objects, emotions, and relationships present.
5. Present the creative challenge: Create a Tableaux Repreaux, act out a reproduction of this historical moment, frozen in time.
6. Pose the creative constraints
   - Ten minutes to create
   - No movement

- No sound
- Use any props available in the room to add detail and meaning
- Work in teams of two, three, or four, depending upon the moment

7. Provide ten minutes for students to design their Tableaux Repreaux.
8. Conduct a showcase for feedback, critique, and sharing of intentions.
9. Take photo documentation of each Tableaux Repreaux. Ask students to write an explanation of these photos in either a Google Doc or on their blogs where they may be shared with a wider audience.

TAKEAWAY

Tableaux Repreaux challenges students to think kinesthetically and visually at the same time. While it lends itself to more literal thinking, more successful Tableaux Repreaux push students to demonstrate layers of intention, considering the composition of the scene, the point of view from which a scene might be portrayed, and the emotions present. Using their bodies to create these scenes also provides opportunity for empathy, to experience in a living still frame what these historical figures went through in their time.

APPLICATION

Science Demonstrate simple machines in action, moments of scientific discovery, or the various relationships of the natural world.

ELA Portray the climactic scene of a novel, the central conflict of a film, or the setting of a short story.

Health and Physical Education Illustrate proper weightlifting or exercise techniques, effective ways to deal with peer pressure, or proper social etiquette.

AMPLIFICATION

- Evolve the Tableaux Repreaux into vignettes with brief dialogue and action.
- Use a digital mark-up tool, such as ThingLink, to annotate photos of Tableaux Repreaux with links to historical information, primary-source documents, and the like.

Chronological Choreography

#IntentionChoreography

60 minutes

TARGET

Depict a timeline of events through a choreographed dance. Use rhythm, movement, and music to capture the defining moments—both historical and emotional—of each point in the timeline.

Chronological Choreography asks students to identify factual, historical information, place that information in proper order, and use a kinesthetic and musical means to convey the information, the sequence in which they occur, and the emotions present in those moments. Students must work within the creative constraints of an observable dance, musical accompaniment, no spoken language, and a three-minute run time.

PATHWAY

1. Watch the trailer for Thodos Dance Chicago's 2013 production of ***A Light in the Dark***, a one-act dance that tells the story of Helen Keller and Anne Sullivan (bit.ly/2thodoslight). Ask students to interpret the action being portrayed.

2. Conduct a Think-Pair-Share.

    - Choose a scene from the trailer.
    - Note, jot, or doodle interpretations of the scene individually. Include specific movements, sounds, gestures, or body language that led to this conclusion.
    - Pair with a partner.
    - Share interpretations and scenes. Work together to clarify and resolve any misunderstandings or confusing moments.
    - Choose one of the two interpretations and scenes to share with the rest of the class.
    - Share and discuss.

3. Watch one of the short clips from the Helen Keller collection on Biography.com [bit.ly/2helenkellerbio]. Ask the pairs to revisit their work in the light of this new information and adjust their interpretations if necessary.

4. Discuss the dance, what the movements seem to be depicting, and how the dancers use physicality to convey meaning.

5. On the board, collaborate with students to construct one or two timelines of historical events from their current unit of study, i.e., the events leading to the start of the American Revolution, the space race of the 1960s, or the discovery of the Watergate scandal.

6. Present the creative challenge: Choreograph a dance of no more than three minutes to demonstrate an understanding of the facts, chronological sequence, and emotional experience of that event.

7. Pose the creative constraints:
    - Three-minute run length
    - Use music provided (See Amplification)
    - Observable dancing
    - No spoken language
    - Work alone or in teams of two or three

8. Provide ten to fifteen minutes for students to design their Tableaux Repreaux.

9. Conduct a showcase for feedback, critique, and sharing of intentions. Record dances for posting and reflection on blogs, websites, or portfolios.

TAKEAWAY

Chronological Choreography challenges students to think of rhythm, movement, and song as tools for expressing understanding. Students must find ways to pantomime the actions of an event, while using the intensity of the movements to express the emotions of the timeline. Students develop empathy for some of the figures of their past, while learning the difficulties choreographers face aligning movement to music to very deliberate intentions and specific outcomes.

APPLICATION

Science Tell the story of continental drift, the migratory patterns of birds, or the lifecycle of a hurricane in dance.

ELA Choreograph the climax of ***The Crucible***, the opening chapter of ***Great Expectations***, or the timeline of ***Out of the Dust***.

World Language Showcase the process of visiting another country for the first time, the challenges of acquiring a new language, or the pathway from immigrant to citizenship in movement to music.

AMPLIFICATION

- Bring a professional choreographer to class to teach the basic techniques of dance construction. Apply those techniques to the dance.
- Collaborate with students in another school to create choreography that must be streamed in real time through video conferencing. Consider how the space between the schools and the display of the screens can be used to convey meaning.
- Incorporate audience participation into the dance. Add a component of students teaching others the dance and the reasons behind the movement into the experience.

CREATIVITY IS PIERCING THE MUNDANE TO FIND THE MARVELOUS

BILL MOYERS

CATALOG OF CRITICAL CREATIVITY:

CREATING WITH STUFF

Oreo Challenge

Board Game Remix

Book Stack Summary

Metaphorical Architecture

Five Course Meal

Metaphorical Fashion

Brick-a-Book

Oreo Challenge

#IntentionOreo

30 minutes

TARGET

Create a visual representation of a concept from the course using any available materials and a single Oreo cookie. Think of it as an advertisement of an idea and try to excite the viewer into wanting to engage with the content of this course.

The Oreo Challenge asks students to identify the most essential content or characteristics of a class, content, or concept, and then visualize that understanding through a variety of media in a way that appeals to a given audience. Students must work within the creative constraints of one circular, multi-textured, and highly malleable object (the Oreo cookie) and may enhance their creative expression with the use of other media, such as modeling clay, plastic bricks, paper, colored markers, etc.

PATHWAY

1. Ask students to complete designer Bob McKim's "Thirty Circles" design exercise. Allow two minutes to transform a page of thirty empty circles. This exercise inspires students to think about things that are generally circular or spherical, though some will opt to take greater leaps in their thinking. Note: It is best to refrain from showing students an example. It is okay for them to be messy in this thinking. Encourage students to think as intuitively as possible in order to keep within the limited time frame.
2. Distribute index cards, one per student. Ask students to label "Side A" and "Side B."
3. Conduct a Think-Pair-Share.
   - Three minutes. "What do you find interesting and/or enjoyable about this class? Fill 'Side A' with notes, jots, and doodles."
   - Three minutes. "What things did you learn that are the most memorable or

intriguing?" Fill 'Side B' with notes, jots, and doodles."

- Students pair with their partners and share their thoughts. Ask students to choose one note, jot, or doodle from each side to share with the class, for a total of four notes, jots, or doodles from that partnership (two from Side As, two from Side Bs).

- As ideas are shared, students may add to their own index cards.

4. Present the design challenge, "How might we use something mundane (a single Oreo cookie) to advertise this class to next year's students?"

5. Pose the creative constraints for this challenge:

    - May be a single image with text or a thirty-second video

    - Must use an Oreo cookie in the advertisement

    - May only use one Oreo cookie UNLESS partnered with another student. Students may then use two Oreo cookies.

    - May use any other materials provided by the teacher

6. Provide three minutes for students to doodle and storyboard their ideas before distributing the Oreos.

7. Set loose their creative mojo for ten minutes as they create their advertisements. (It is helpful to offer a heads-up warning after about five minutes and just before the ten-minute mark.)

8. Conduct a gallery walk or showcase of the advertisements, including student critiques and explanations of intentions. If students maintain blog portfolios, ask them to include images of the process and final product and contextualize with their creative reasoning.

TAKEAWAY

Oreo Challenge promotes ***divergent thinking*** by giving students a common problem to solve within the boundaries of ***creative constraints***. Limiting the timeframes pushes students to invent solutions in a hurry. Requiring students to use an Oreo encourages innovative uses of available materials and "outside-the-cookie" approaches.

Students practice ***visual and metaphorical thinking*** as they develop their idea. Creating an effective advertisement demands students appeal to an authentic audience. This exercise allows for ***metacognition*** as students reflect on the resonant aspects of their course experience.

APPLICATION

Science Advertise the laws of motion, the cellular reproduction cycle, or the theory of evolution.

Social Studies Advertise a political candidate from the past or present, a controversial law or policy, an abstract concept (communism or expansionism), or a historical event.

Health and Physical Education Advertise healthy lifestyle choices, fitness plans, or sporting events.

AMPLIFICATION

- Distribute the advertisements online or in print form to reach both the intended audience as well as others who may find delight and joy in seeing students' creativity.
- Teach students the three classical forms of appeal: character (ethos), emotion (pathos), and reason (logos). Have them apply one or more of those forms to their advertisement.
- Publish the advertisements and interview a "focus group" about their effectiveness, just as an advertising agency would do. Apply the feedback and create new iterations.
- Adjust your audience from next year's students to this year's parents and guardians. This can be a powerful way for students to build empathy for their parents and guardians, while engaging

the folks at home in their students' thinking. The work could also be shown on parent night or at student conferences.

- Use as an introductory activity at the beginning of the course to spark interest in the content. Ask students to randomly choose something from their course resources or a topic from the syllabus. They must then conduct independent research to find out enough about the concept in order to illustrate it.

- Instead of facts, ask students to illustrate questions.

- Team up with a group of students from a different department (e.g., seniors with first graders) and conduct a joint Oreo challenge.

- Shifting the task from "advertise" to "illustrate" opens up more possibilities, while keeping the benefits of divergent thinking intact. Apply this challenge to any content or concept in any classroom.

crayola
CASTLE
tube.
GAMING

faceb
k

Board Game Remix

#IntentionGame

90 minutes

TARGET

Remix the objectives, rules, game pieces, and game play from at least three board games to demonstrate understanding of a given plot line, process, or journey.

Board game Remix asks students to identify the stages in a plot, the steps in a process, or the benchmarks in a journey, while demonstrating an understanding of the relationships between each point on those timelines and the challenges and conflicts encountered from point to point. By adhering to the creative constraints of using multiple board game sources, publishing the remixed rules and gameplay, and explaining intentions behind each aspect of the game, students have to move away from ***Candy Land***-chance and simplistic "answer the question and move three spaces" formats to more complex and meaning-driven gamification.

PATHWAY

1. Make three columns on the marker board and label them as Word Games, Strategy Games, and Chance Games. Distribute sticky notes and ask students to identify as many board games as they can that fit in those categories in three minutes. Include only one game example per sticky note.

2. After populating the columns, work with students to assess the success of the sorting. Facilitate a discussion of the difference between word games (***Scrabble***, ***Upwords***, ***Apples to Apples***), strategy games (chess, checkers, ***Monopoly***), and chance games (***Chutes and Ladders, Candy Land, Hungry Hungry Hippos***). Some games may belong to more than one category, and that is okay—take the opportunity to discuss the features that move those games out of a single category.

3. Break the class into groups of one, two, or three students. Ask each group to choose one

of the games from the board and write down everything they know about the following aspects of the game.

- The Objective of the Game (The Goal)
- The Pieces Involved in the Game (The Tools)
- The Way in Which the Game Is Played (The Play)
- The Rules the Players Must Follow During the Game (The Rules)
- Before embarking on this work, complete the work as a class for one of the games. Keep on a timer of five minutes. Part of the exercise here is noticing what sticks, what we remember as being important for a certain game, and what is not.
- Provide five to seven minutes for the groups to take down these notes. It may be helpful to create a graphic organizer to manage the information. Circulate and answer clarifying questions. Try to hold back from giving students the answers—again, it is all about what we have remembered and what we have not.

4. Jigsaw new groups of three or four students each. The intent here is to get a variety of different games represented.
5. Pose the ten-minute challenge: Remix and mash up your games into a brand-new game. Determine the objective of the game, the pieces you will need, the basic game play, and the rules. Finally, it must have a name. You must complete this in ten minutes and be prepared to record a two-minute video in which you explain it to the rest of the class.
6. After ten minutes, give each group two minutes to record their presentations and upload their recordings to the class Google Drive or YouTube accounts. These do not need to be finished productions—the recordings are to document their thinking and work for future reference and formative assessment. Alternatively, you may have one or two groups share their work, with others sharing their work in a future class.
7. Present the formal challenge: In groups of one, two, or three students, demonstrate your understanding of the process, the journey, or the plot line we have been studying by remixing at least three board games into a

new game where the objectives, the pieces, the gameplay, and the rules represent the key information and concepts we have been studying.

8. Provide time for students to design their board game remixes. Suggest they use those four aspects of the games—objectives, pieces, gameplay, and rules—to help them organize their thoughts.

9. Allow students access to a collection of board game pieces and materials gathered from thrift stores and yard sales, so they may learn and create by physically experimenting and discovering inspiration.

10. Upon completing board game remixes, ask students to document intentions by recording group members playing the game and explaining how the game's design reveals the deeper understandings of the process, plot line, or journey studied.

 TAKEAWAY

Board game Remix requires students to think beyond the basic facts of a process, plot line, or journey, and look deeper at the challenges faced in moving from point to point along those timelines. By remixing well-known board games, students discover the elements of gamification throughout our life experiences and how treating challenges like a game may reveal solutions. Taking time to craft rules and boundaries also makes students more aware of the difference between authentic and arbitrary limitations. Why make this harder? Just because it should be hard or because there is a reason? Why not allow all players to go at the same time? Why do we take turns? What might this simulate? Games can be tremendous opportunities to explore systems thinking and construct new ways of looking at input, outputs, and variables.

APPLICATION

Health Remix games to demonstrate understanding of patterns of addiction and ways to break those cycles. Challenge students to transform childish games into the serious work of healthy lifestyles and breaking habits.

Science Mash up games to demonstrate food chains and ecosystems, evolutionary progress and natural selection, or soil erosion and landform development. Challenge students to represent complex patterns that are affected by many factors and could have many different outcomes.

ELA Design games to emphasize the roles conflict and characterization play in the development of a plot. Challenge students to focus less on the events of the plot line and more upon the motivations behind the characters, the sources of conflict, and the impact of resolving those conflicts.

AMPLIFICATION

- Mash up collectible card games, such as ***Pokémon*** or ***Magic: The Gathering,*** to create games that can evolve over the course of the school year. Consider how booster decks and expansion sets might be created as new units are explored.

- Code video-game remixes based on early Nintendo and Atari games using tools such as Scratch. Consider how video-game remixes might make the games more portable and how portability might be part of the game play.

- Develop publishable-quality games and challenge students to market them to other classrooms and students. Consider how raising the stakes of having others play the game to demonstrate their understanding requires more thoughtful attention to the accuracy of the gameplay.

Book Stack Summary

#IntentionStack

30 minutes

TARGET

Craft a summary of a film, video, or presentation by arranging a selection of books such that their titles summarize the content.

Book Stack Summary asks students to determine key details, important events, and central ideas of audio/video content and then summarize those findings. They must do so within the creative constraints of limited language (only the book titles available), physical representation (arranging a stack), and a ten-minute time limit.

PATHWAY

1. Prior to the activity, set up the following.
    - Work with the school librarian to set up a location for this activity and identify a selection of books to use. As interesting, engaging, and effective as this activity can be, it can also make a mess of a library in a hurry. Ask the librarian to determine the best way to clean up at the end of the experience.
    - Create an example using a well-known film that students are likely to identify (***Star Wars***, ***Finding Nemo***, ***Harry Potter***, etc.) and have it waiting for the students upon arrival.
2. Distribute index cards. Ask students to create three columns, label one with a question mark, one with a dollar sign, and one with a light bulb.
3. Ask students to fill these columns with timestamps and jots, notes, and doodles as they watch. Emphasize the importance of the timestamps as there will be time to go back to those moments and review the video.
    - Question Marks. Anything that requires clarification or raises bigger questions.
    - Dollar Signs. Anything that seems like an important detail that should be remembered.

- Light Bulbs. Anything that feels like a new understanding, a new realization, or an "aha" moment.

4. Play the video as students take notes using the system described above. If possible, provide students access to the video on their own devices for review after the whole class watches.

5. While students add more detail to their notes after the watching, distribute sticky notes.

6. On the board, make three columns: question marks, dollar signs, and light bulbs. Ask students to select one observation from their notes for each column, put it on a sticky note, and then put it in the proper column on the board.

7. As a class, look for trends and outliers in the sticky notes. Explore answers to questions students have.

8. Bring the index cards to the library, where the example stack is waiting for the class to interpret. Work as a class to identify the example stack's source of inspiration.

9. Present the Creative Challenge: Create a book stack summary of the video.

10. Pose the Creative Constraints:

    - Ten-minute time limit
    - Only the book titles available
    - The books must be arranged so the titles are clearly visible

11. Put ten minutes on the clock while students build their summaries. Encourage students to try multiple iterations and seek inspiration from their notecards.

12. Conduct a showcase of the stack summaries with students sharing their intentions and choices. Ask students to document their stacks with photos and to then capture their thinking on a blog or Google Document.

TAKEAWAY

Book Stack Summary challenges students to express understanding through a combination of limited vocabulary and physical representation. Those limitations require that they consider the connotations and associated meaning of their diction, that they account for an audience and how their words will be perceived, and that they build with intention rather than convenience.

APPLICATION

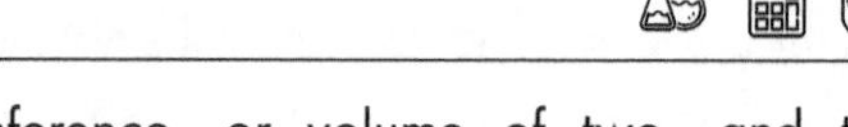

Science Watch TED Talks on nanotechnology and artificial intelligence, listen to episodes of WNYC's ***RadioLab*** on science and ethics, or examine documentaries on genetically modified foods and global warming and distill these complex ideas and positions into Book Stack Summaries.

Mathematics Build Book Stack Summaries to convey the order of operations for solving a given problem, to explain how to calculate area, circumference, or volume of two- and three-dimensional figures, or to capture a mathematician's contributions to the field.

Visual and Performing Arts Watch three stagings of ***Romeo and Juliet*** Act I, listen to three covers of Stevie Nicks' "Landslide," or three productions of Tchaikovsky's ***The Nutcracker*** and create Book Stack Summaries that distinguish each production from the next.

AMPLIFICATION

- Shift the intention from summary to review, evaluating the quality of the content through a book spine stack.
- Rather than using book spines, try the same approach with DVDs or Blu-Ray discs, music CDs, or video games, perhaps even food packaging or junk mail.
- Challenge students to conduct debates using Book Stack Summaries to express their positions and rebuttals.
- Explore examples of Book-Spine Poetry online and across social media. Experiment with placement and location, time, and space of the book titles. Consider building digital collages, stop-motion videos, or short films to capture the construction.

THE ALOHA SHIRT
HOBBS
ANYTHING BUT ORDINARY
Korman
BORN TO ROCK
HYPERION
ROSOFF
HOW I LIVE NOW
DE LA CRUZ
Lost in Time

Metaphorical Architecture

#IntentionArchitecture

120 minutes

TARGET

Design a piece of architecture—whether home, museum, school, theater, landmark, or another structure altogether—to represent the essential features and/or relationships within a given topic, concept, or unit of study. Create a model of the design to represent three-dimensional thinking and determine how the design would exist in actual space.

Metaphorical Architecture asks students to think about the content they are learning in terms of the homes in which they live, the institutions where they attend school, and the landmarks they visit. While the creative constraints may vary with regards to materials, time, dimensions, or features, in any Metaphorical Architecture challenge, the student must be able to identify the central understandings and vital features of the content in order to create a meaningful design.

PATHWAY

1. As a warm-up, revisit the meaning of ***metaphor*** and its importance in communicating complex ideas.

2. Play this analogies game: Ask each student to write down at least one abstract noun (e.g., peace, creativity, love) and at least one concrete noun (e.g., horse, California, mobile phone) on a sticky note. Students should post to the board or wall in separate columns (this can also be done digitally with a collaborative spreadsheet document). Next, students must choose one abstract noun and one concrete and form an analogy. They may find it easier to work in small groups and then share with the rest of the class. For example, ***How is love like a mobile phone?*** Perhaps the fact that it "lights up" when energized? Maybe the concept of different apps creating meaning for the whole resembles what we look for in a love match?

Does the fact that we feel comforted by it and secure strengthen this analogy, and that if it gets damaged or lost, we feel distraught? Are we always in search of a "new model"? Now ask students to draw an image that depicts the analogy they identified. Each student or group should try to describe and draw at least one analogous relationship and then share to the class for discussion.

3. Explain that we are used to seeing metaphor in visual art, poetry, and literature, but that design and even architecture can be centered around these symbolic depictions as well. If you have younger students, you can perhaps bring up the Statue of Liberty and discuss how a tangible object was made to depict an abstract concept. Older students might want to explore the history of modern metaphoric architecture, particularly in iconic structures, such as the **Sydney Opera House** and the **Lotus Temple** in New Delhi. The **Ribbon Chapel** by Hiroshi Nakamura is also a prime example, as a wedding chapel built around the concept of two lives, twisting and turning until they become one in marriage.

4. Introduce the challenge. Students will design (and potentially construct a model of) a building, monument, or other architectural space (such as a park or train station) that reflects the essence of an abstract concept. Examples of abstract concepts should ideally come from the curriculum and can be political or social ideals, emotions, vocabulary words, scientific processes, and the like. The key is to translate the nuanced idea into something—a space or structure—concrete and symbolic. Remind them that a hamburger stand shaped like a hamburger is slightly metaphorical, but they should seek to extend the metaphor into something that addresses more of the context, hidden meanings, and connotations of the topic. It should help the process if their chosen concepts are already abstract.

5. Students may use a variety of mediums to design and/or build their model. They can start on paper with a two-dimensional design then move towards digital mock-ups or three-dimensional structures made from plastic bricks, clay, wood, cardboard, etc. Encourage them to start with a brainstorm of ideas about the characteristics of their chosen concept.

Ask them to continue by thinking about what physical and architectural elements would signify these aspects? For example, large windows might symbolize transparency, openness, enlightenment, vulnerability, fragility, etc. They should think about:

- The shape of the exterior of the structure
- The surrounding environment (which is part of the architecture)
- The materials used to make the structure
- The interior and all its facets (decorative elements that are part of the structure, for example)
- The name of their design

6. A large part of the assessment should be how students are able to justify their creative decision making and process. What is the reasoning that went into their choices? How do the various facets of their structure articulate the nuances of their abstract concept?

TAKEAWAY

Metaphorical Architecture challenges students to think about representational intentions in terms of not only visual design and aesthetics but also materials, location, and even geography. Students develop complex systems of symbolic meaning, contributing and building patterns of meaning just as they will need to identify and analyze in other contexts. Students practice the art of using architectural features to convey meaning and in so doing, better understand buildings and spaces in their lives.

APPLICATION

ELA Design a metaphoric piece of architecture that depicts the relationship between two literary characters, an example of literary conflict (such as "man versus nature" or "man versus society"), or a major theme in a chosen novel. Design a building that illustrates a poem in a tangible way. Use vocabulary terms as inspiration for the metaphoric design.

Social Studies Design a metaphoric piece of architecture based on a major concept in the curriculum, such as a social or political philosophy. Design a monument or other space that pays tribute to a war or other tragic or significant incident in history. Use a culture as inspiration for the design, paying careful attention to the various traits of that culture. Design a monument or other space in tribute to an important historical figure.

AMPLIFICATION

- Make this challenge interdisciplinary by involving physics, math, design, tech, art, history, and language classes, each developing a piece of the criteria.
- Hold a design showcase fair and open it up to the wider school and local community. Share physical models and provide a narrative explaining them.
- Involve parents in the profession or local architects, interior designers, landscape artists, and furniture designers as guest speakers and mentors for this project.
- If your school has a 3D printer, use that resource to make designs tangible.
- Build a website or faux Wikipedia entry for the design, showing each part in detail and offering the philosophy behind the design choices.

Five-Course Meal

#IntentionMeal

Varies (Depends upon food-preparation time.)

TARGET

Prepare a metaphorical dinner party to demonstrate understanding of a process.

Five-Course Meal asks students to identify the key stages in a process and express their understanding of each stage and its relation to the overall system, through the creation of a multi-course meal. Creative constraints include requirements that the meal must feature as many courses as there are stages, steps, or phases in the process. The costs must stay within the teacher-defined budget limit. Any preparation constraints the teacher may impose because of kitchen-access issues. And it may be created by a team of one, two, or three student chefs.

PATHWAY

1. Distribute copies of the school cafeteria menu for the week, a local restaurant menu, and/or a weekly nutrition health plan from a hospital nutritionist.

2. Ask students to code the menu. "Put a dollar sign next to everything that appeals to you in this menu. Put a question mark next to everything that doesn't sound particularly appetizing to you. Put an exclamation mark next to everything that you will avoid at all costs."

3. Conduct a Think-Pair-Share. Ask partners to share their coding with one another and then choose one from the dollar sign, one from the question mark, and one from the exclamation mark categories to share with the rest of the class. Ask the class to prepare to explain the reasons why they coded these items the way they did.

4. Facilitate a brief, "You Are What You Eat" activity.

    - Column A. List three things you've eaten this week.

- Column B. List three things you've done this week.
- Column C. List three of your personality traits.
- Column D. List three things you love.
- Now try to connect the dots across all four columns. How might what you've eaten connect to what you've done, to who you are, to what you enjoy? How might what you've eaten remind you of one of your personality traits or something that you love? For example, bean and rice burritos stuffed with roasted veggies and sour cream and ***salsa fresca*** remind me of how I have so many varied interests, how I crammed a ton into my Tuesday, and how I love feeling comfortable in my own skin.

5. Set that metaphorical thinking aside for a moment and distribute index cards.
6. Ask students to doodle whatever process the class has been studying in five minutes or less. Emphasize the importance of labeling each step in the process sequence. This will help organize their thoughts when they get into the meal planning.
7. Present the challenge: Prepare a metaphorical meal where each course represents a stage in the process we are studying.
8. Pose the creative constraint.
    - Work in teams of one, two, or three chefs.
    - There must be as many courses served as there are steps, stages, or phases in the process.
    - The cost of preparing the meal must stay within the stated budget.
    - All courses must be made in the given time and must use the given kitchen resources.
9. Provide time for students to plan their meal.
    - Distribute enough index cards for each student to have one per course in the meal. Label "Side A" and "Side B."
    - On Side A of the card, students doodle, note, and jot the foods that each phase suggests, i.e., metaphase in mitosis reminds me of Twizzlers and challah bread because of how the chromosomes twist

about and line up along the middle.

- On Side B of the card, students use online grocery stores or a local supermarket's website to determine costs to make their meals. Teachers should plan on providing kitchen staples—baking soda and powder, corn starch, flour, sugar, salt and pepper, cooking oil, etc.
- Encourage the use of menus, cookbooks, documentaries, food writers, professional chefs, and restaurant owners as sources of inspiration.
- Once students have their intentions set on the number of courses, the food to serve and why, and a rough budget, teachers should sit and review with students each budget and their preparation plans.

10. Shop for food and establish a kitchen space for students to prepare the meal.
11. Provide time for students to create, document their intentions with photos if not video and voiceovers, and then present their meals. Challenge them to continue thinking about their intentions as they create and document any additional thinking and connections they make as they are preparing the meal.
12. As the class circulates to each meal, encourage tasting and require student chefs to explain their intentions.

TAKEAWAY

Five-Course Meal challenges students to think in terms of extended metaphors. These sorts of higher-order comparisons build semantic connections and become heightened by the tactile experience of preparing food. The budgetary constraints might be seen by some as a limitation; instead, the constraint can be seen as an opportunity to practice divergent thinking, to research, and to experiment with alternative approaches.

APPLICATION

Science Lay out a spread inspired by the scientific method, species classification, or the water cycle.

ELA Serve up a writing process, a plot structure, or a poetry analysis buffet.

World Languages Feed the class a verb conjugation, a dialogue, or a study method.

AMPLIFICATION

- Bring a food-service professional to class to help prepare the meal and show students how even the cooking techniques themselves might be part of the metaphor.
- If creating and serving the food is a barrier, design just the menu. Do so in the shape of a professional restaurant menu, with descriptions of the courses included on the menu itself. Consider how design features of the menu, i.e., color, font, texture, etc. may contribute to the metaphor.
- Use ethnic foods or dietary considerations as creative constraints.

Metaphorical Fashion

#IntentionFashion

60 minutes

 TARGET

Design a metaphorical line of clothing based on an essential theme evident in the current unit of study. Whether a series of slogan T-shirts, ironic trucker hats, or a complete runway show of meaningful formal wear, students must develop wearable means of expressing thematic understanding.

Metaphorical Fashion asks students to determine patterns of meaning, symbolic representations, and overarching ideas, representing content knowledge through clothing. They must work within the creative constraints of the materials available with knowledge that the garments are intended to be worn. These are to be designed for catalogs and runways rather than costume shows and carnivals.

 PATHWAY

1. As a warm-up, ask students to take a couple of minutes and survey the other students in the room and notice ways in which fashion choices tell stories. If your school requires uniforms, there could be other indicators of individualism, such as footwear, accessories, make-up, bags, etc., though you could ask students to look through magazines, search the Internet, or access their photos on social media for examples. Discuss these examples, reminding students to maintain respect and refrain from any negativity. Reiterate that fashion has always been a mix of form and function and is often used as a means of self-expression. You might want to ask students to describe examples of their favorite items of clothing and what they "say" about them as individuals or to share their most memorable "message" T-shirt or hat.

2. Explain that many fashion designers draw influence from other disciplines, such as history, fine art, politics, the natural world, and technology. It is also common in lower-

cost "ready-to-wear" lines to feature slogans and other text reflective of the zeitgeist or current events. In more recent history, "trucker hats" and baseball caps readily display pop-culture quotes or allude to political and social views. A quick search on the Internet will yield some interesting examples, so you might wish to have students locate and share one to a collaborative digital space or create a brief slide deck of your own.

3. Introduce the challenge. Remind students what a metaphor is and discuss the specific criteria you have selected for this project. Students may design a metaphorical fashion collection of several pieces based on a theme, one or more "ironic" T-shirts that may include plays on words such as puns, or a hat with a message. Ideally they can draw the designs using analog or digital tools, contextualize them by explaining their reasoning, and then physically create a prototype. It is perfectly fine to leave out the prototyping and focus on the two-dimensional design. Students may also find it appealing to work with a partner or in a small group, perhaps developing an entire line of clothes, accessories, and wearables around a theme.

4. ***Tips for ideating:*** Ironic T-shirts and hats often feature puns and plays on words, so students should first make a list of relevant concepts, people, and vocabulary in the discipline and then think of rhymes or homonyms that would work (for example, ***"math puns are the first SINE of madness,"*** or ***"weapons of mass percussion"*** for band). They can also think of ways to remix existing pop-culture phrases, such as ***"When in Rome, do as the Visigoths,"*** or ***"New Deal With It."*** When designing a fashion line, students can think about color and its symbolism, the line and structure of the garments, and motifs and patterns that have significance to the topic. A collection based on a novel might include quotes from characters embedded in the fabric, whereas one based on the planets in the solar system might feature hues representative of each planet and jewelry signifying the moons or rings.

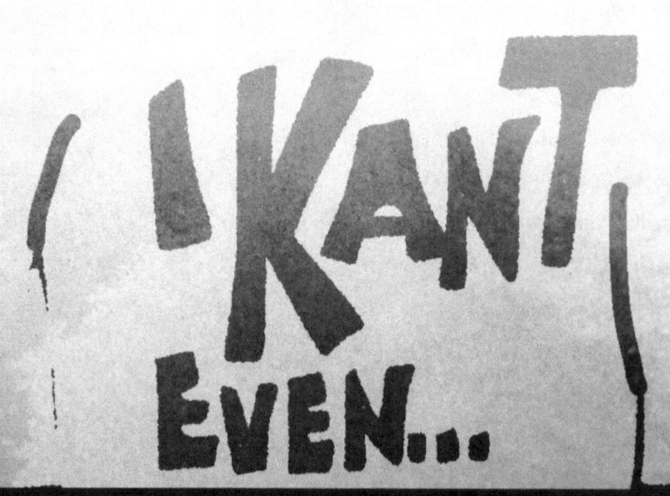
I KANT
EVEN...

TAKEAWAY

Through the creation of wearable meaning, Metaphorical Fashion challenges students to think in all three dimensions, as well as factoring shape, proportion, and movement into their intentions—even if they do not create actual garments. Wordplay and irony, color, and texture have equal value in these designs, revealing opportunities for layered meanings and purposes. Furthermore, students uncover the hidden stories our wardrobes reveal and explore the potential power of personal appearance.

APPLICATION

Visual and Performing Arts Use music genres, art genres/movements, or famed artistic works as inspiration. What would a fashion line based on Vivaldi's ***Four Seasons*** look like? What slogans would an ironic T-shirt collection based on the Impressionist artists feature? Drama students could develop costuming for an original play or series of monologues or use message hats as prompts for improvisation.

Science Use geographical phenomenon or the planets as inspiration for a thematic fashion collection with special attention to color, texture, and motifs. Put environmental studies into practice by using found objects and other recycled matter as the construction material for garments and accessories. Experiment with items from the hardware store to see how this challenge can reinforce design tech or physics studies.

Social Studies Focus on an era, culture, or subculture. Capture the zeitgeist. Translate a political or philosophical statement or ideology. Incorporate famous persona or quotations. If studying psychology, use the nuances of emotions as inspiration—what would a collection based on "envy" or "melancholia" look like?

AMPLIFICATION

- Build a website for the fashion line and practice photography, design, and/or coding skills.
- Hold a fashion show featuring all the student designs and invite local fashion-industry leaders, parents, etc., to judge.
- Film a "making of" documentary, tracing the process of the design and construction, complete with interviews of students describing their intentions and troubleshooting.
- Create animated GIFs of all the designs in a collection.
- Do a magazine-inspired photoshoot of the designs (with student models) and create a printed 'zine or poster series.
- Create a short television advertisement parodying those of major fashion lines.

Brick-a-Book

#IntentionBrick

45 minutes

TARGET

Summarize a passage, article, or chapter of text using LEGO bricks, Jenga blocks, or any other building set to create a metaphorical representation of the ideas present in the text.

Brick-a-Book requires students to identify the key details and central themes of a text in order to create an effective summary. While students may want to focus on concrete details and literal interpretations, the creative constraints of a timeframe and limited materials require them to use more conceptual, metaphorical representations.

PATHWAY

1. Distribute index cards. Ask students to label "Side A" and "Side B."
2. Give students three minutes to jot, note, or doodle their day thus far on "Side A."
3. While students doodle their days, distribute small piles of building bricks on each desk.
4. Provide students five minutes to create a representation of one moment in their day so far using just the materials on their desk.
5. After the time is called, allow students to circulate the room and see the various ways individuals chose to build their days. Encourage questions and discussion; suggest they look for clever and interesting approaches such as using minimalism, abstract shapes, or not connecting the bricks at all.
6. Conduct a brief discussion of what was made and seen.
7. Distribute a short article related to the current unit of study, or ask students to produce a recent reading from class.

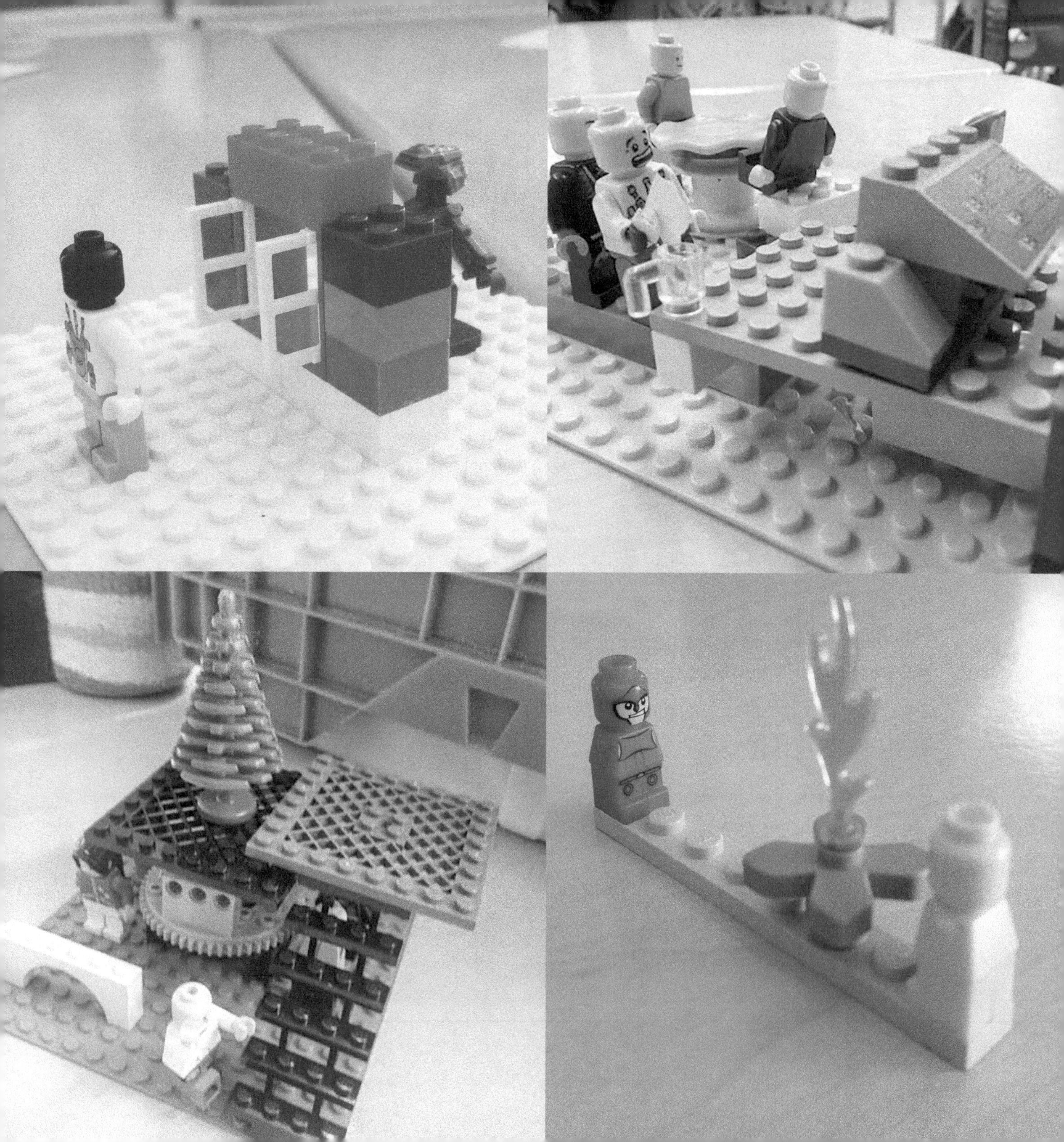

8. Ask students to flip their card to Side B and to jot, note, or doodle the key ideas from the text, while the text is read aloud. Provide three minutes after the read-aloud for students to continue making notes on Side B.

9. Present the creative challenge: Create an effective summary of the reading using building bricks.

10. Pose the creative constraints.

    - You must start with the bricks on your desk.
    - If you want more bricks, you must swap, trade, or borrow from another student by asking.
    - Ten-minute time limit.

11. Provide students ten minutes to complete their build.

12. Ask students to find a partner with whom to share their build.

13. As students share with one another, request they find one interesting feature or detail about their partner's build and summary that others should notice.

14. Facilitate a round-robin of sharing and discussing the details of the reading and the intentions behind the various builds. Look for trends, insights, and outliers to point out common strategies and unique approaches to the problem.

TAKEAWAY

Students must apply multiple layers of critical thinking to complete Brick-a-Book. They must begin with accurate raw information and self-assess the extent to which they have identified and evaluated the most important specifics from the source text. They must apply divergent thinking and see multiple solutions within limited resources and creative constraints. They must justify their choices and explain their intentions to an audience, while also determining information worth sharing with an even larger audience.

APPLICATION

Science Construct the chapter on plate tectonics with LEGO bricks, an editorial on self-driving cars with Jenga blocks, and an article on space archeology with Erector parts.

Mathematics Build explanations of the Pythagorean theorem in Keva planks, the quadratic formula in DUPLO bricks, and the area of a circle in K'nex rods.

World Languages Fashion the conjugation of a verb in Bristle Blocks, the architecture of a culture in Lincoln Logs, and the pattern of a dialogue in Mega Bloks.

AMPLIFICATION

- Design representations using donated arts and crafts supplies, natural materials from the school campus grounds, or clean trash and food wrappers gathered during a lunch period.

- Acquire sets of littleBits or Snap Circuit electronics to add movement, sound, and light to the builds, engaging other modalities, representations, and metaphors.

YOU ARE
A
MASHUP
OF
WHAT
YOU
LET INTO
YOUR
LIFE
AUSTIN
KLEON

CATALOG OF CRITICAL CREATIVITY: CREATING WITH SOCIAL MEDIA

HashMash

One Word to Rule Them All

Character Gallery

Gif Story

Volley

Fauxial Media Profiles

Belief Board

HashMash

#IntentionHashMash

15 minutes

 TARGET

Mash up content knowledge with allusions and references to pop culture, common experiences, and school life to create hashtags that demonstrate understanding.

HashMash draws upon students' prior knowledge, both academic and social, to make connections to the current content. Puns, wit, humor, and associated meanings distinguish successful HashMashes from lesser so. Apply the creative constraint of 140 characters (per Twitter) and a ten-minute time limit, so the HashMashes may be shared and crowdsourced.

 PATHWAY

1. Ask students to make a list of musical artists and bands they enjoy or know.
2. Then ask students to make a list of ideas related to school, such as recess, testing, late passes, detentions, etc.
3. Direct students to mash up the bands with school and apply the hashtag #schoolbands at the end. Provide these examples: UNo.2Pencil #schoolbands, Student Led Zepplin Conferences #schoolbands, or Florida Georgia Line Up for Recess #schoolbands.
4. Put two minutes on the clock for these #schoolbands.
5. Conduct a brief Think-Pair-Share. Ask pairs to choose one #schoolbands to share with the class.
6. Work with the class to brainstorm important information about the current unit of study. Make a list on the board.
7. Present the creative challenge: Create a HashMash called #[Insert Unit of Study Here]Bands, i.e., #NutritionalBands, #GrammaticalBands, or #WeatherBands.

8. Pose the creative constraints.
    - May only be 140 characters long, including the hashtag
    - Ten minutes to create
9. Ask students to log on to Twitter or Instagram. If students are not able to access social media, log in to a class account on a teacher device.
10. Circulate as students create, and ask them to explain their intentions. As students demonstrate initial success, challenge them to choose bands and content that seem to have more than one reason to go together. For example, Student Led Zeppelin Conferences references a nontraditional approach to portfolio reviews, just as Led Zeppelin represented a new approach to rock and blues when they came on the scene.
11. Encourage students to post their HashMashes on social media, and ask them to follow the hashtag to see others.
12. Conduct a showcase of HashMashes to uncover student intentions and discuss the references students made.

TAKEAWAY

Though a shorter experience than other critical-creativity activities, HashMash challenges students to synthesize ideas from two contexts and unify them. Successful puns and allusions require a deeper understanding of both the content and the reference than just surface knowledge. Posting the HashMashes on social media asks students to be vulnerable, to publish their thinking to an audience, and to look to others for inspiration and collaboration.

APPLICATION

ELA Mash up food with elements of fiction in #EatingStories, sports with poetic devices in #JerseyVerse, or automotives with essay composition in #WritingandDriving.

Social Studies Mash up movies with government studies in #HollywoodVotes, video games and geography in #GameMaps, or children's literature with psychology in #SeussianPsyche.

Health and Physical Education Mash up restaurants with digital citizenship in #OnlineDining, apps with fitness planning in #MobileWorkouts, or the military with substance abuse in #DrugWars.

AMPLIFICATION

- Collaborate with students in other classes in real time and asynchronously by sharing the HashMash tag with colleagues around the world.
- Create GIFs or memes to accompany the HashMashes to add a visual component and another layer of intention.
- Ask students to invent their own HashMashes and deliver a series of mashups on social media.

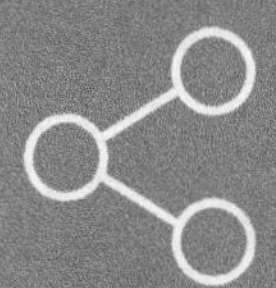

One Word to Rule Them All

#IntentionOneWord

15 minutes

TARGET

Distill something complex, such as an experience or content knowledge, into a single word and augment that word using metaphorical typography and/or accompanying doodles.

One Word to Rule Them All provides the ultimate creative constraint. It forces students to think about what, to them, is their greatest takeaway from a learning experience. It asks them to "sum up" something complex, which refines their communication skills. One Word asks students to identify the denotative and connotative meanings of a word, weighing the associations of language against literal definitions. They practice both metaphorical and visual thinking and are challenged to make the abstract concrete.

PATHWAY

1. As a warm-up and introduction to metaphorical typography, students may design their names. Ask them to think about their name as their DNA. Inquire if they are familiar with "Google Doodle" and how designers at Google create specially crafted typography for certain events, like holidays or the birthdays of famous individuals at google.com/doodles. First, they should handwrite their name as they would normally sign it. Ask them to consider if their signature shows any characteristics that might characterize their personality. Then challenge them to write some adjectives that describe their personality (switch it up by doing this as a partner activity). Finally, they may experiment writing their name in three different typefaces that allude to aspects of their personality. Encourage them to include accompanying doodles, similar to the Google Doodle project. Ask students to share with the class or with a partner or small group, explaining their creative choices.

d i s t R A c t i o n
8/10/15
#ONEWORD
@amyburvall

2. Tell students the aim of this challenge is to distill a complex thing, such as a lesson, idea from the content, or feelings they have about something they've learned, into one word only. They will then attempt to write that word using metaphorical typography, in which the lettering "tells the story" of the various nuances of the word.
3. After completing their words, they may share them to their blogs or other archiving tool as well as present to the class, sharing their intention.

TAKEAWAY

One Word to Rule Them All challenges students to go deeper in their thinking and develop layers of intention to justify what seems like a simple choice. In the process of choosing a word, students evaluate the denotative and connotative meanings, narrowing the possibilities down to that single word that best captures their thinking. Designing the word's appearance requires still more consideration. Whether in comic books or advertising, typography carries meaning and purpose well beyond its visual appeal. Examining features, such as kerning and spacing, typeface, and font size, helps students to think deliberately about appealing to an audience in all written endeavors. One Word asks students to question the unintentional messages they may be delivering with a poor font choice.

APPLICATION

Visual and Performing Arts Use the word as a springboard for lyric composition, dance choreography, a piece of visual art, a poem, or monologue. Distill a play or sum up a character in one word. Condense each scene in a longer play into one word. Summarize an art movement or an artist's style in word. Then reference that in the typography and surrounding doodles.

TENSE
2/27/15
ONE WORD
@amyburvall

Health and Physical Education When studying various diseases, use the one-word technique to sum up the nature of the illness, or incorporate the one word into a public service announcement aimed at prevention. Athletes can choose one word to describe how they felt about their performance or use an inspirational one word as their mantra when participating in the sport.

World Languages Words can be written in the target language to reinforce vocabulary skills. Pronounce the word or vlog in the target language about the word and why it was chosen to represent the learning experience.

AMPLIFICATION

- Use the analogies on the Metamia site metamia.com for inspiration and try to sketch the analogies made from the words, such as "chemistry is an Impressionist painting." Alternatively, make up original analogies and depict those as metaphorical typography.
- Keep a One-Word diary for each day or lesson as the course progresses. Underneath the word, written in metaphorical type, write a brief explanation as to why that word symbolized the learning moment. After an accumulation of words, reflect on what the word choices say about the experience of the course. The diary can also be digital (like a blog) and words can be shared on social media. Consider compiling those words into a yearbook or digital publication students may use to remember class or reignite learning in the future.
- At the end of a unit or other learning period, all students can create a one-word representation of their greatest takeaway and post as a collaborative grid in the room. Discuss differences and commonalities.
- Create an animation or other type of video with the one-word choice. Speedsketching, in which the entire process of drawing is captured by the camera from a bird's-eye view and then sped up in the editing process, is a technique that would lend itself well to this challenge.

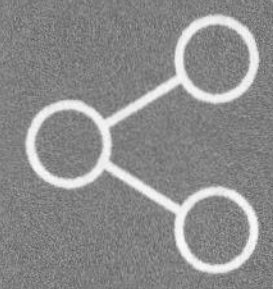

Character Gallery

#IntentionGallery
60 minutes

TARGET

Curate an online art gallery to represent the characterization of a given individual whether fictional, historical, or contemporary.

Character Gallery requires students to demonstrate knowledge of character development—personality, physicality, beliefs, values, etc.—and the ways in which those aspects of one's self are revealed through storytelling—speech, thoughts, effect on others, actions, and looks (STEAL). Students must look at the information available to make these conclusions and explain how a piece of artwork conveys these findings. Apply the creative constraints of three curated items, sourcing items from online galleries of reputable art museums, explanations of intentions, and a twenty-minute time limit.

PATHWAY

1. Direct students to the online galleries of several museums including one of local, national, and global prominence. Ask them to find one or two pieces there they find appealing.

2. Conduct an "Identity Card" experience.

    - Distribute index cards and label "Side A" and "Side B." Divide Side A of the card into six boxes and label the quadrants as follows: Personality, Physicality, Values and Beliefs, Goals and Dreams, Fears and Worries, and Hmmm.
    - Thinking about yourself, doodle, jot, or note descriptors of yourself in those categories.
        - Personality (e.g., outgoing, shy, reckless, careful, etc.)
        - Physicality (e.g., 5'5," green eyes, tiny thumbs, etc.)
        - Values and Beliefs (e.g., tolerance for other points of view, free will, religious principles)

- Goals and Dreams (e.g., to be published one day, to own a home, to ride a camel, etc.)
- Fears and Worries (e.g., spiders and snakes, getting lost, nothing good to eat at lunch, etc.)
- Hmmm (i.e., descriptors that don't seem to belong anywhere else)

- Flip the card over to Side B and make another set of six boxes, labeling this set: Speech, Thoughts, Effect on Others, Actions, Looks, and Hmmm.

- Thinking about yourself still, doodle, jot, or note how someone might learn about your character traits from interacting with you.

  - Speech: Things you say
  - Thoughts: Things you think
  - Effect on Others: Things you cause others to feel
  - Actions: Things you do
  - Looks: Things you wear (even your hair)
  - Hmmm: Things that don't seem to have a category

3. Think-Pair-Share: You as Art

   - Five minutes. Return to the online museum galleries and find a work of art that connects to one or more of your descriptors or behaviors. Prepare to explain your choice to another.
   - Pair with a partner to share what you found and the intention behind this choice.
   - Choose one of the two pieces of art and an explanation to share with the rest of the class.

4. Distribute new index cards.

   - Ask students to create an identity card—both front and back—for one of the characters/individuals they have been studying recently.

   - Ask students to include page numbers to text and/or six-word references "[First three words of quoted text] . . . [last three words of quoted text]" to support their claims.

5. Present the creative challenge: Curate an online art gallery that represents the identity of a character/individual we have been studying.

6. Pose the creative constraints.

   - Must choose three items from a reputable art gallery's online collections to represent aspects of the character/individual's identity

   - Must include brief explanations (curator's notes) of which aspects of identity the items represent and which characterization methods reveal this. These notes must include page numbers and/or six-word references "[First three words of quoted text] . . . [last three words of quoted text]."

   - Gallery and explanations must be posted online using Padlet, Pinterest, and/or a blog

7. Provide time for students to curate their galleries and compose their curator's notes.

8. Conduct an online gallery walk. Ask students to provide meaningful feedback to each curator as each curator shares his or her intentions.

TAKEAWAY

By comparing artwork to characters in Character Gallery, students are able to make metaphorical connections between visual information and text-based information. Students also develop stronger understanding of character development, having constructed a gallery based on those understandings. Role-playing as curators provides students an entry point into how art galleries and museums are shaped. And publishing the galleries online allows authentic audiences to provide feedback, while also learning from the students' work.

APPLICATION

ELA Build a collection for the supporting characters of ***Romeo and Juliet***, for one of the Transcendentalist poets, or each protagonist from a thematic collection of short stories. Name the gallery exhibition with a line from one of the works studied.

Social Studies Curate a collection representing Greek philosophers, World War II military leaders, or twenty-first-century social justice advocates. Seek art from the eras of those individuals or require students to use art outside of those timeframes.

Health and Physical Education Design an art museum around athletes who broke color barriers, chefs who innovate cuisine, and doctors who revolutionize medicine. Embed video of those figures in action that mirrors the art piece chosen.

AMPLIFICATION

- Practice empathy by choosing a collection of pieces that character may hang in their home. Justify each choice.
- Create a piece of original artwork inspired by the three pieces curated. Represent all three chosen aspects of identity in that one piece of artwork. Document the intentions behind the piece with a video walkthrough of the art piece.
- Focus on a single artist, finding three pieces by that artist that represent the character in question. Then conduct an investigation into the artist and research biographical information, professional skills and accomplishments, and personality traits and beliefs. Compare and contrast the artist to the character based on evidence and determine whether or not the three pieces found that represent the character may also then represent the artist. Present the findings.

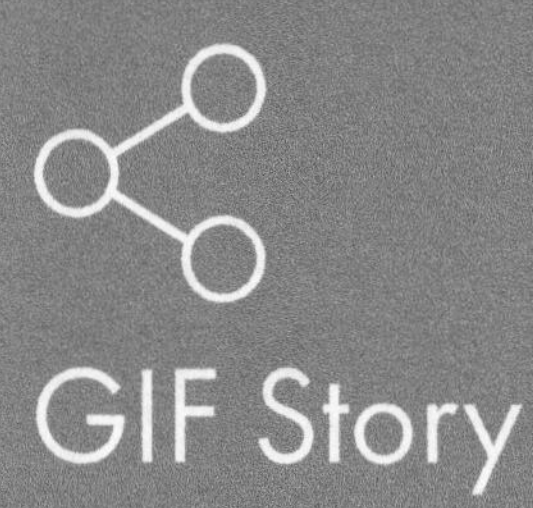

GIF Story

#IntentionGIFStory

45 minutes

TARGET

Use a series of animated GIFs to tell a story that incorporates content knowledge and/or personal experience.

GIF Story challenges students to use animations created from films, television, games, and other media and apply them to expressing emotions, illustrating conflicts, and conveying a series of factual events.

PATHWAY

1. Warm up by asking students to write down an emotion on an index card. Encourage them to write more complex emotions than "happy" and "sad," though it is fine to identify an emotion they might feel on a daily basis, such as stress, frustration, or relief. Collect all the index cards and explain that they will be used for a short game of charades.

2. Ask for student volunteers to come up to the front of the classroom. Each should draw one of the cards and try to act it out in a short scene or with as much facial expression and appropriate body language as possible. If students are apprehensive about performing in front of the class, you could do this in partner groups, with partners acting the word out for each other after you call it out.

3. Explain that emotions are a powerful tool in storytelling, as is the use of metaphor. This challenge requires consideration of both, as students explore the use of animated GIFs in articulating knowledge.

4. Ask students what they know about animated GIFs (Graphics Interchange Format) and how they are used. For example, most social media sites allow the embedding of GIFs, and they are featured as a choice on some keyboards.

Twitter links to a bank of GIFs with an "add a GIF" button that searches common human feelings, such as "do not want," "I don't know," "eye roll," and "you got this." Our media is allowing us to become increasingly visual in our communication, and GIFs are similar to emojis in that they convey much nuance with simple imagery.

5. Students might have a favorite GIF to share, or you can ask them to search for a GIF on giphy.com that shows how they are feeling at the moment. If students are on Twitter, they can Tweet out a message with a GIF from the Twitter GIF search.

6. Discuss that while most people use a single GIF, a string or combination of GIFs can be used to tell an effective story. Students can practice this by thinking about their daily routine, such as awaking and getting ready for school, taking a test in a class, playing a sport, hanging out with friends, or relaxing at the end of a long day. Ask them to find GIFs that convey their feelings for three distinct periods of their day.

7. Challenge the students to apply this GIF storytelling to your content. Guide them in choosing something relevant to depict, reiterating that they want to focus on the emotion experienced in the action as the "story" progresses.

8. Students can share their GIF stories as a slide presentation or in a blog post, making sure to explain their reasoning behind their choices.

TAKEAWAY

GIF Story asks students to determine the most effective tools for telling a story from a wide range of possibilities. Narrowing those possibilities and evaluating their value requires students think critically about the subject of the story, not only in this instance, but in future cases where a student has to determine the best tool for a job. Furthermore, when using GIFs, students familiar with both the original source material and the content knowledge are better able to find nuances and angles that make for something greater than the sum of its parts.

APPLICATION

Social Studies Tell the story of a historical event as it unfolds in a linear fashion with a series of GIFs. Trace the life of a relevant historical figure with a selection of GIFs, emphasizing the potential feelings that person had as they progressed through specific life events. Use GIFs to share sentiments about current events.

Science Use GIFs to illustrate an experiment. Personify scientific concepts and systems and assign GIFs as analogies.

ELA Illustrate the story of a novel from the perspective of one of the characters using a string of GIFs. Using a series of curated GIFs, write poetry to contextualize each one. Use literary devices, such as irony, hubris, paradox, metaphor, or tone, as the basis for the GIF story.

AMPLIFICATION

- Rather than using found GIFs, students can create their own animated GIFs using existing or original footage. Some students might want to make GIFs with artistic elements, such as modeling clay, plastic bricks, or drawings. There are numerous tutorials and apps that facilitate DIY GIFs.
- The challenge can be collaborative, with each student in a group adding to the GIF story. This could be extended globally via social media with students working with peers from other schools.
- Use the challenge as a warm-up or "do now" prompt: Write some inspiration from the content on the board or project on a screen with the caption *"________is like . . . ."* Students have a few minutes to respond with a GIF and explain their reasoning.
- Create a thematic website, blog, or other digital community for your course and allow students to post GIFs that relate to the content. These can be single GIFs rather than "GIF stories."
- Encourage students to use animated GIFs to articulate their feelings about their work. This can be a poignant tool for reflection if students explain their intention.

Volley

#IntentionVolley

30 minutes

TARGET

Create visual and verbal metaphors by exchanging ideas back and forth with a collaborator and building upon one another's contributions.

Volley asks students to collaborate with others as they demonstrate content understanding through a series of back-and-forth creative interactions. Each variation on the volley poses its own creative constraints, while all of them require students build upon the work of another, embracing the improvisational spirit of "yes, and." Students must also use visual and verbal metaphorical thinking to present their interpretations and perspectives.

PATHWAY

1. As a warm-up, ask students to write a vocabulary term from their unit of study or a concept learned in the course on a piece of paper. Then ask them to wad the paper up into a "snowball" and, given the signal, throw it across the room to someone. After the snowball fight, make sure every student has a paper with a word. Challenge them to visualize the concept by drawing an icon or image of the term on the paper. At this point, you can discuss the difference between a literal visual interpretation and a metaphorical one (which will involve more critical thinking). After a time limit of three minutes or so, ask students to share their examples and describe the reasoning behind their sketch.

2. Remind students that ***creativity works best with constraints***, and sometimes those constraints may be provided by another party, thus throwing serendipity into the mix. This challenge is a lot like a volleyball game or, if continued, like a tennis match. A peer will "serve" up a prompt to be answered with a creative response.

3. The following are some ideas for volley:

    - ***Visual Verse:*** One person offers another an original poem (can be content-related), and the other responds with a relevant image. The image may be found or an original created from the student's choice of media. Or, flip it with the first student providing the image and the second student responding with verse.

    - ***Blimage:*** A portmanteau of "blog" and "image" (you can also do "blideo" with video), one student offers an image prompt that inspires a blog post, essay, or other type of prose penned by the recipient. To get more perspective, the writer can "tag" others to respond to the same image. It is best if the image lends itself to metaphorical thinking, or at least make the point that this should be aimed for in the writing (many thanks to Steve Wheeler @timbuckteeth for starting the first blimage with Amy).

    - ***VizVo Volley:*** "Vizvo" stands for "visual vocabulary." Developing a visual vocabulary for important concepts and terms will help students remember what they learn (check out Allan Paivio's "dual coding" theory of cognition). Class and individual notes become richer when students can develop an image bank of icons representing knowledge. In VizVo Volley, one word is posted, and all students can sketch a visual icon for that term. Or, a number of words may be posted in a row, and students can draw their image responses on sticky notes and create rows of their interpretations. Take time to discuss the reasoning behind their images and the differences and commonalities apparent in the collection as a whole.

    - ***Hashtaggerie:*** This volley plays with the "rigorous whimsy" concept. Keeping in mind that hashtags serve to further contextualize a piece of media or information, students develop complex and clever hashtags based on an image provided by the other student (found or made). Alternatively, the first student may offer a hashtag based on some aspect of the content, and the recipient can

Erin Olson
@eolsonteacher

slowly tapping Nevermore
knocking-pendulum passing
enter House-ill dark
beware the Eye that
traps & torments
revenge that curses &
consumes

create the image. Challenge students to use plays on words, mash words together in interesting ways, develop true portmanteaux, and offer critique or opinion about the topic within the hashtag. An image created as a response to a hashtag should strive to depict the various nuances of the tag.

- ***Headline Riff:*** This volley includes two to four students. The first student finds an interesting headline. This could be from the newspaper (great for historical studies), from an article related to the content, from a chapter in a textbook, etc. The second student responds in writing to the headline. This could be in prose, such as an article or journal entry, or as poetic verse. The third student (or back to the first), records an audio track influenced by the headline and text. Students can do voiceovers, create music tracks, or ambient noise tracks. The fourth student (or back to the second) creates a visual relevant to the work—a photograph, artwork, animation, or video. To make the work required in this volley somewhat equal, each student could do all four parts and exchange with the next in a round-robin style.

TAKEAWAY

Growing from the adage, "None of us is as smart as all of us," Volley challenges students to build upon the ideas of others in order to create original material that demonstrates content knowledge. While they might participate in several short volleys—they do not have to take long—each experience develops students' ability to collaborate in meaningful ways. Every volley becomes a puzzle to solve and a riddle to answer. Students also learn that creative expressions can be quick and meaningful, as well as long-term and purposeful, and the more content knowledge you develop, the more you can contribute.

APPLICATION

Visual and Performing Arts Use famous works of art as the prompts for ***Hashtaggerie***. Act out a response to ***Blimage***. Use original artwork as a response to ***Visual Verse***. Write an original musical score for ***Headline Riff***.

Social Studies Use historical newspapers or a current event headline for ***Headline Riff***. Use portrait paintings, battle scenes, and other artwork as prompts for ***Hashtaggerie***. Create a bank of icons the class can use in notes for ***VizVo Volley,*** or use the icons to annotate the textbook or other readings.

World Languages Write text for ***Blimage*** in the target language. Create a ***visual vocabulary*** with new vocabulary terms. Write a poem in the target language for ***Visual Verse***.

AMPLIFICATION

- Leverage social media channels for all of the volley challenges—students can work with other classes in geographically distant schools, or they can partner up with a specific peer and exchange elements for the volley. Or, students can play with the world at large, for example, offering a hashtag challenge for ***Hashtaggerie*** and asking their network to participate.
- Instead of individuals acting as participants in the volley, a team of students can volley with another group.
- Volley with another age group or subject area in your school. Small children's drawings, for example, would be wonderful inspiration for older student's poetry.
- Produce a book or ebook with the ***Hashtaggerie*** or ***Visual Verse.***
- Use the ***Headline Riff*** challenge to create movie trailers and hold a film festival.

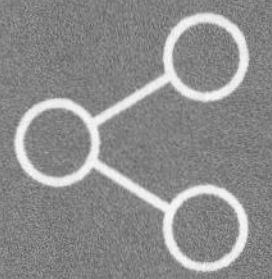

Fauxial Media Profiles

#IntentionFauxialMedia

45 minutes

TARGET

Create faux Facebook, Snapchat, Instagram, or Twitter parody accounts to demonstrate factual content knowledge, as well as the ability to adopt another voice and point of view.

Students really need to "get inside the head" of their subject in order to create a nuanced social media presence, including images, language, and design that matches the subject of the parody.

PATHWAY

1. Conduct a quick poll with students regarding their use of social media platforms. One suggestion is to create posters for several of the most well-known platforms (Twitter, Facebook, Snapchat, Instagram, YouTube, Pinterest, LinkedIn, etc.) and place them around the room. Then ask students to place a dot sticker or write a tally mark under the title if they use it. Alternatively, use a spreadsheet, Google Form, or other polling software to record their responses and show the results. Debrief by asking which they prefer and why.

2. Students can then continue by brainstorming some common attributes of these spaces and how people negotiate in them. They can record their ideas on the poster, with sticky notes, or on the digital form. Brainstorming works best when individuals have some time to think for themselves and write their ideas before sharing with the entire group. Ask them to focus on specific characteristics; for example, abbreviations commonly used, popular hashtags such as #tbt or #nofilter, the use of emojis and "likes" or hearts, the recommendations of skills in LinkedIn, the use of RT (reTweet), or the "@" sign when referring to others. This will help them think of things to incorporate in their faux feeds. If possible, allow them to explore some of these platforms during this task.

3. Introduce the challenge and the specific criteria for your content. Students will develop a

parody account and populate it with plausible posts. You can decide if they should stick to one type of platform or choose their own, resulting in a more varied response. Carefully discuss the assessment criteria, perhaps developed with the students as part of the class discussion. For example:

- ***How much factual knowledge should be included?***
- ***To what extent can the posts be satirical? Whimsical? Humorous?***
- ***What is a reasonable range for the number of posts in the parody feed?***
- ***How will students demonstrate understanding of the nuances of the subject?***

4. If possible, show examples of existing parody accounts based on real or fictitious literary or historical characters.

5. Students may create their parody accounts and feeds using digital tools and templates or, if they are younger, in an analog fashion with posters (such as a series of Instagram posts by a character or a Facebook "wall"). There are several faux Facebook, Twitter, and Instagram templates online that can be located with a simple search, or students could be challenged to create their own. Remind them to include the profile page or area with avatar and relevant tagline.

TAKEAWAY

Fauxial Media challenges students to adopt points of view that are not their own in order to create comical, but fact-based parodies of important figures, events, and concepts. Parody best works when it balances the silly and ridiculous with the factual and accurate. Thus, students must apply their working knowledge of social media to ensure these accounts have the look and feel of authenticity. In the process of doing so, students grow their awareness of how social media is an extension of one's self and evaluate the extent to which their own social media is an accurate representation of themselves.

APPLICATION

Visual and Performing Arts Develop social media profiles for famous artists or for the character featured in their artwork.

Social Studies Historical figures easily lend themselves to parody social media accounts. Historical events can be "backchanneled" as a Twitter chat.

Health and Physical Education Personify a concept like a sport, an organ of the human body (when studying physiology), or even a disease or disorder. Challenge students to create personalities, attitudes, and behaviors that align to the concept's essential characteristics.

AMPLIFICATION

- Creating parody accounts on social media platforms allows others to collaborate in the new digital identities of these characters. Followers can respond to posts with additions of their own, participating in the development of the character and often offering insights. Why not collaborate with another class outside your geographical area?

- Set an update schedule for the account, challenging students to continue adding relevant content that demonstrates new learning and engages followers.

- Ask students to use these parody accounts to comment on current events, timely news stories, local issues, and classroom experiences, demonstrating deeper understanding of both another point of view and the topic at hand.

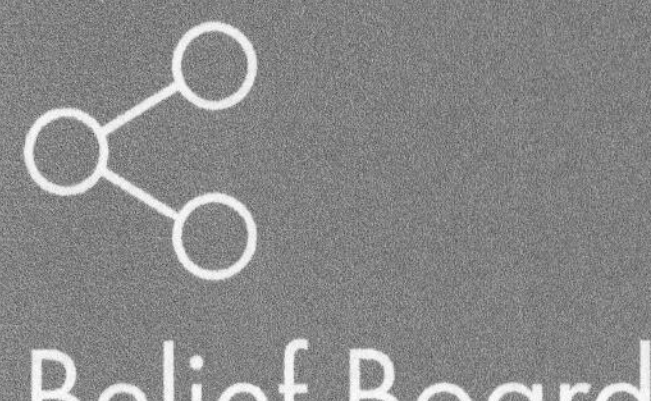

Belief Board

#IntentionBoard

30 minutes

TARGET

Craft a series of belief boards from the point of view of a given individual, whether fictional, historical, or contemporary to demonstrate understanding of that individual's beliefs and perspectives.

Belief Board asks students to empathize with another's point of view, particularly related to values and positions, using quotes, artwork, colors, objects, memes and more found on Pinterest, Polyvore, and other online scrapbooks. Students adopt the voice of their subject, using appropriate diction and applying relevant context to their creations. The creative constraints confine the boards to a focus on the individual's beliefs and a use of first-person point of view for each caption. It also requires students to use evidence to support their assertions.

PATHWAY

1. Prior to class, visit Pinterest and create a board featuring several quotes, a variety of artwork, and a number of memes.
2. During class, display the Pinterest board.
3. Ask a student to choose one of the quotes on the board. Then brainstorm as a class: What if we imagined the person who would put this on their wall? What are they like? What do they believe in?
4. Repeat the process with one of the pieces of artwork and one of the memes.
5. Provide students five minutes to write or record a more developed description of one of these invented characters. Ask students to focus on beliefs and perspectives that individual might have and where the source of those beliefs originates.

6. After providing student volunteers an opportunity to share their characters, present the creative challenge: Create a Pinterest board or Padlet wall that illustrates the point of view and beliefs of one of the characters/individuals we have been studying.

7. Pose the creative constraints:

    - Collect at least one quote, one meme, one piece of artwork, and one other object/color, for a total of at least four pins.
    - Each choice should reveal a belief or perspective this character holds. Write the captions from the character's point of view, explaining why this pin was chosen.
    - Apply evidence from the class text in the caption, including the page number if applicable, to prove this is an opinion the character would assert.

8. Provide time for students to build their boards.

9. Ask students to comment on each other's boards, providing critical feedback and questions. Contribute comments and challenge creators to explain their intentions behind their choices if it is not immediately evident.

TAKEAWAY

Belief Boards challenge students to look at the stew of memes, artwork, graphic design, and more on Pinterest to make connections between those seemingly unrelated ideas and their current readings. They practice greater empathy by adopting a point of view that is not their own. While students are not creating new characters, they are creating new contexts, essentially role-playing these characters in a digital age. Furthermore, students must use evidence to support their claims that these are valid interpretations of the character.

APPLICATION

ELA Develop a pin collection for one of the characters in ***The Giver***, for a modernist poet, or Tennessee Williams' supporting characters in ***Cat on a Hot Tin Roof***.

Social Studies Curate a collection representing early European settlers arriving in North America, politicians in the Age of Glasnost, or current figures running for local, state, or national office.

Science Design a board for a well-known architect, astronomer, or ecologist.

AMPLIFICATION

- Maintain the boards over the space of several weeks, adding more pins from the characters' point of view, one per class period. Document the evolution of the board over time, particularly the explanations.

- Create a community board on Pinterest and collaborate on finding pins relevant to what is happening in class.

CATALOG OF CRITICAL CREATIVITY REFERENCE GUIDE

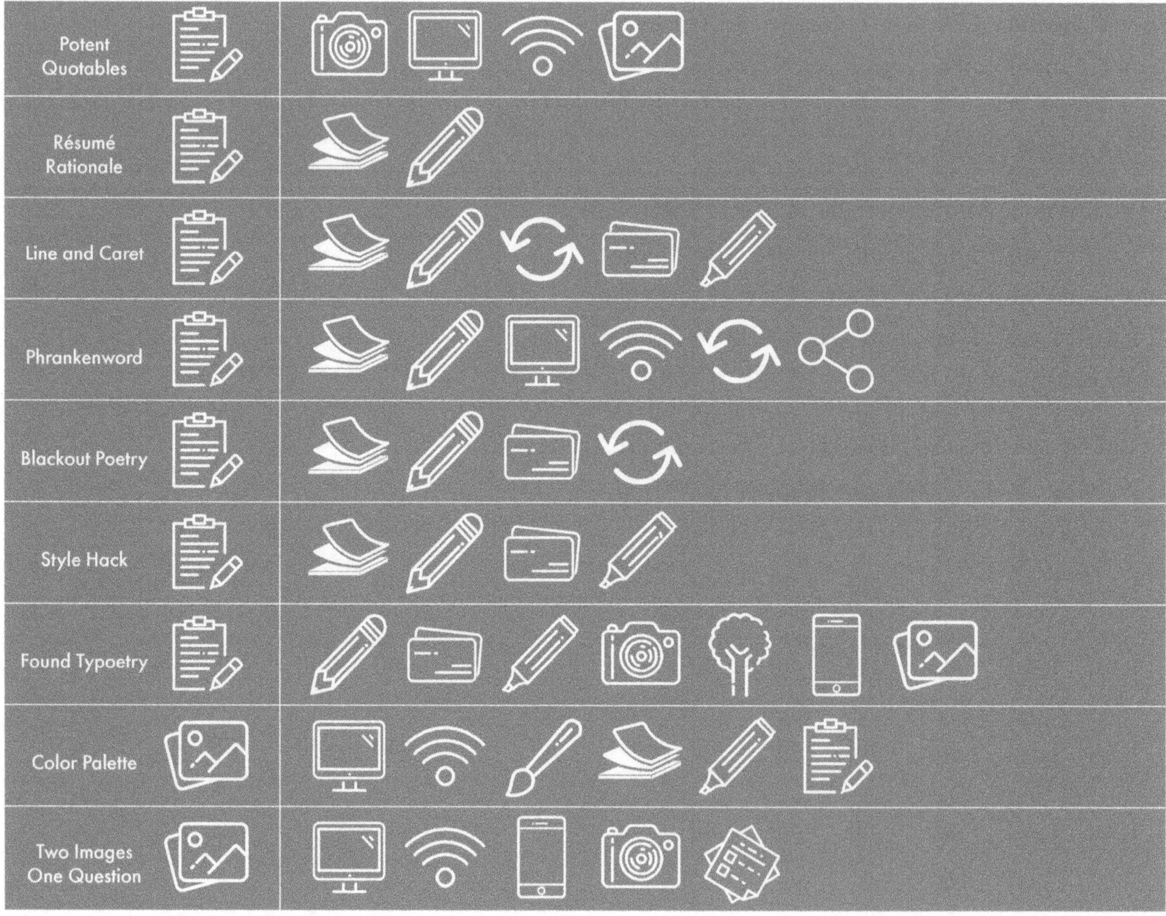

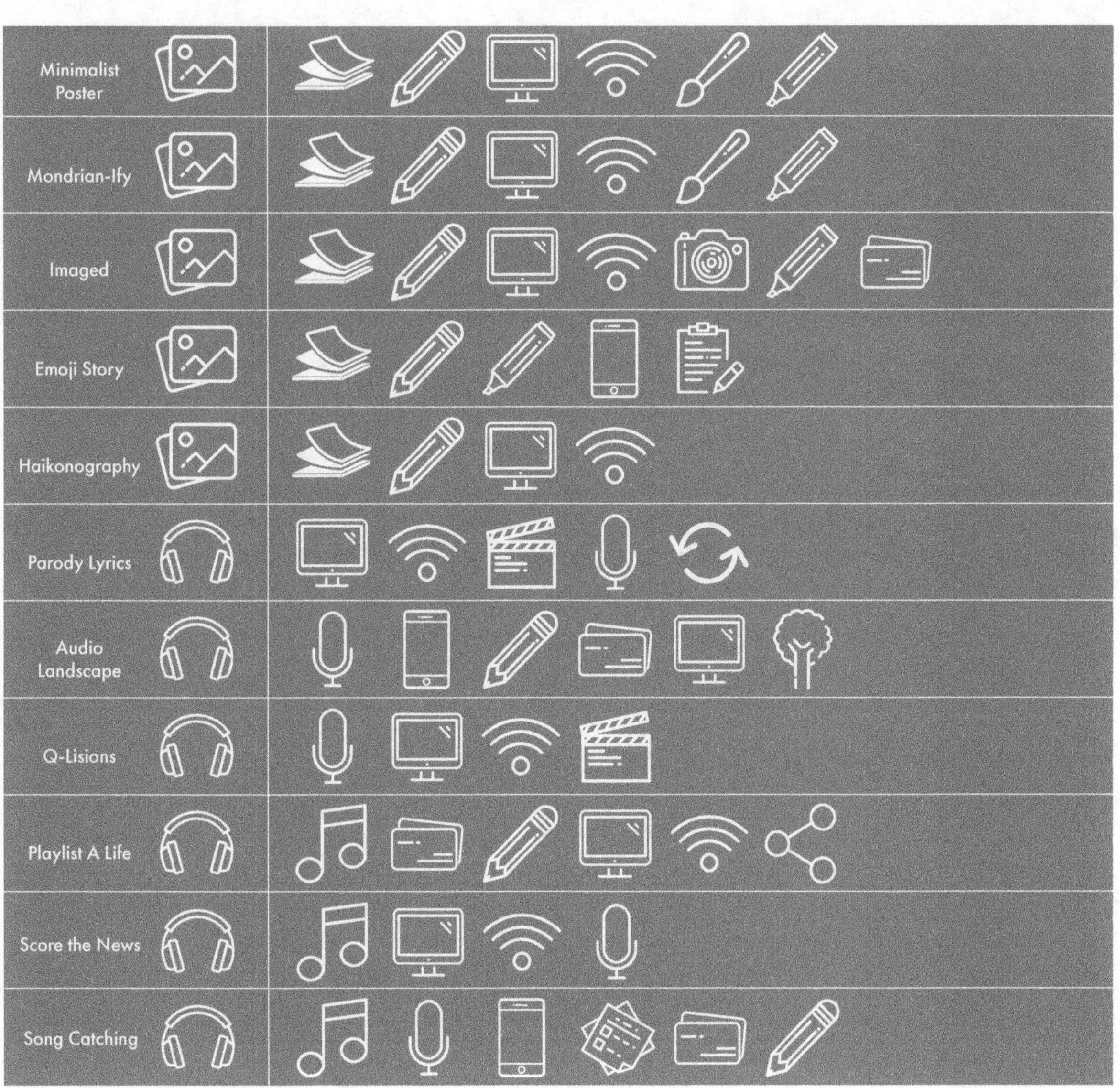
Minimalist Poster
Mondrian-Ify
Imaged
Emoji Story
Haikonography
Parody Lyrics
Audio Landscape
Q-Lisions
Playlist A Life
Score the News
Song Catching

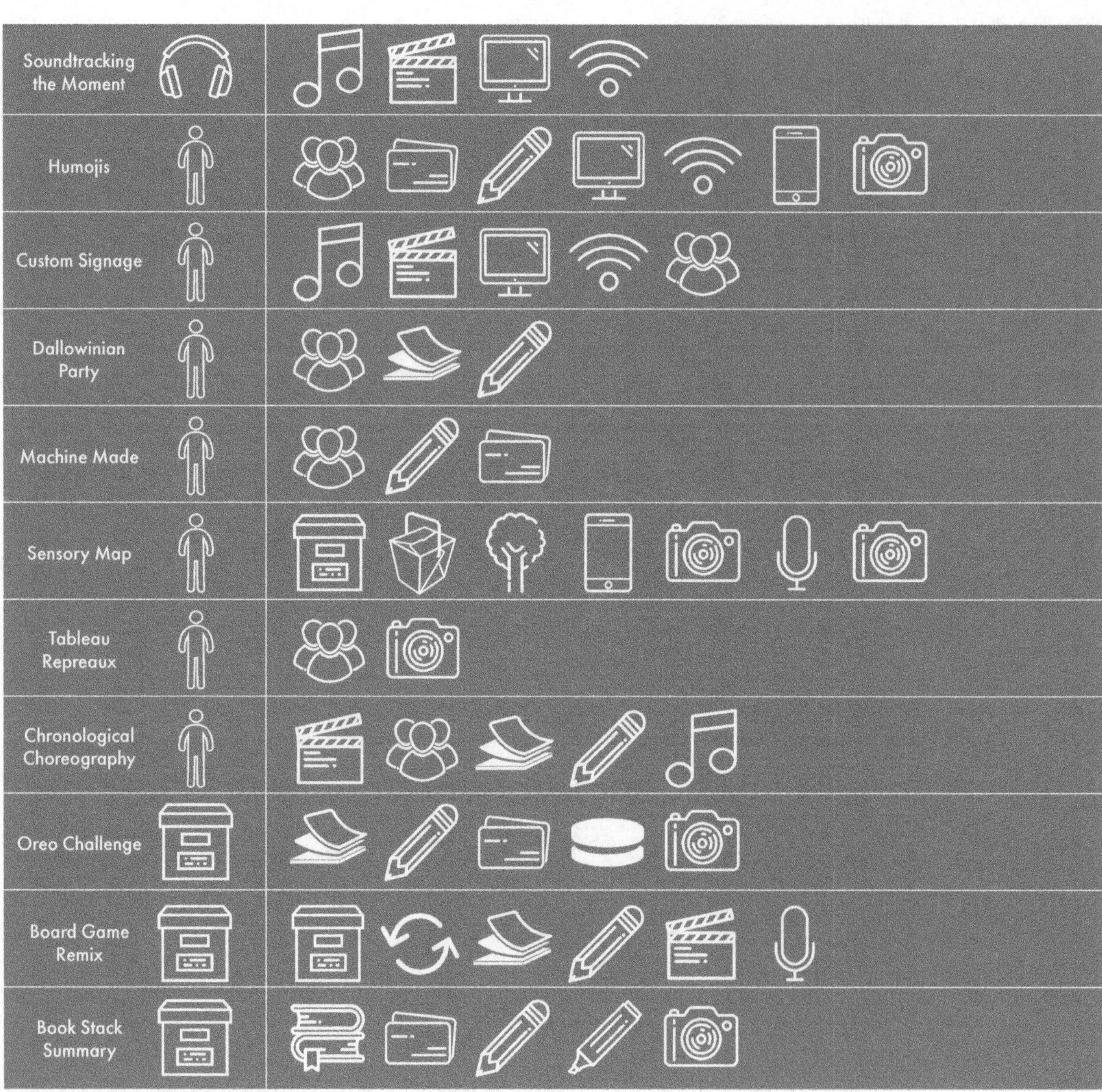
Soundtracking the Moment
Humojis
Custom Signage
Dallowinian Party
Machine Made
Sensory Map
Tableau Repreaux
Chronological Choreography
Oreo Challenge
Board Game Remix
Book Stack Summary

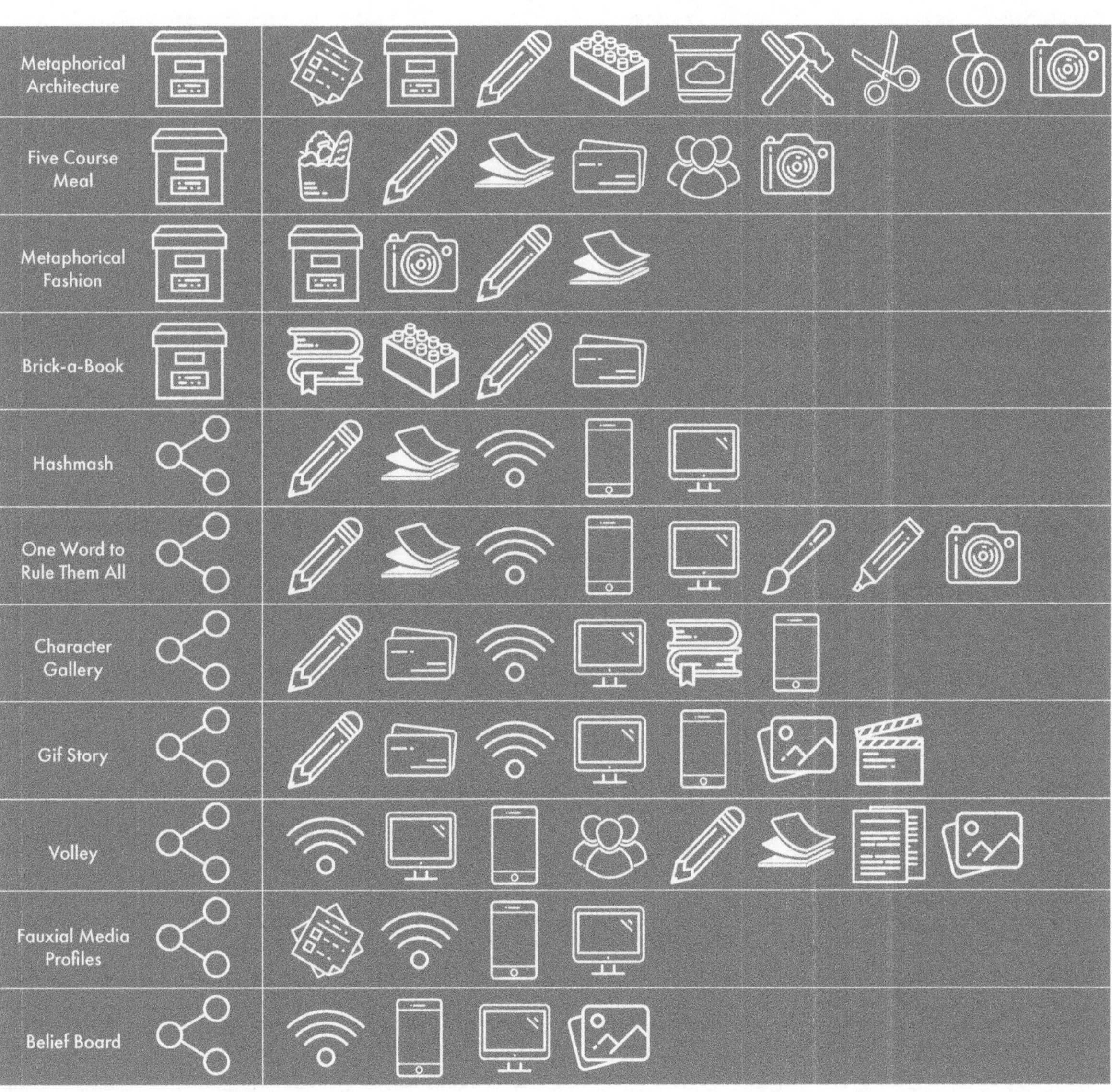
Metaphorical Architecture
Five Course Meal
Metaphorical Fashion
Brick-a-Book
Hashmash
One Word to Rule Them All
Character Gallery
Gif Story
Volley
Fauxial Media Profiles
Belief Board

THERE IS NO WIN
THERE IS NO
FAIL
THERE
IS ONLY
MAKE

JOHN
CAGE

MASHUPS AND REMIXES, COLLISIONS AND EXPLORATIONS

Use the space on the following pages to combine and transform items from the catalog into original explorations and formats. Invent a hashtag for your new idea and share it with us on social media by adding #IntentiontheBook.

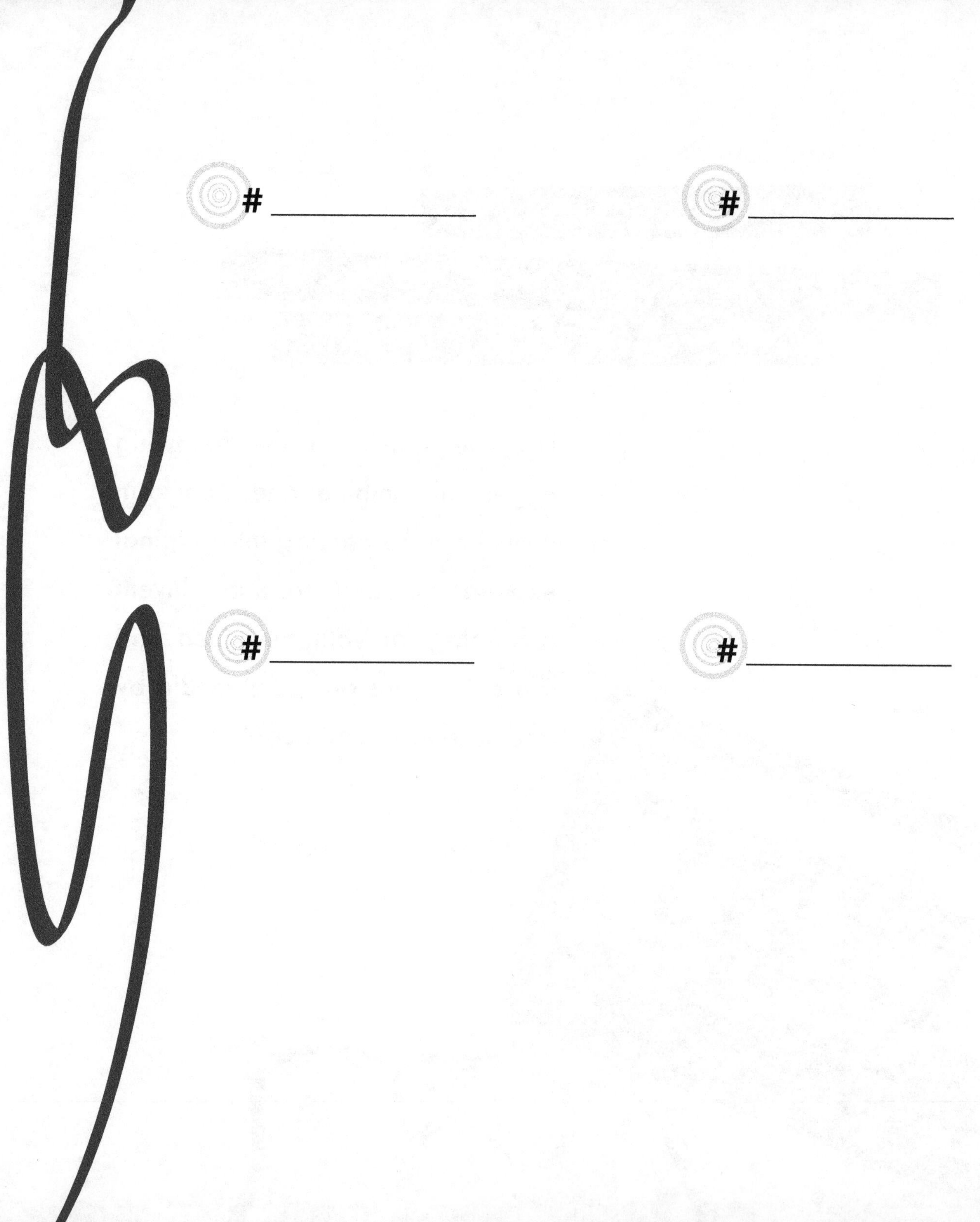

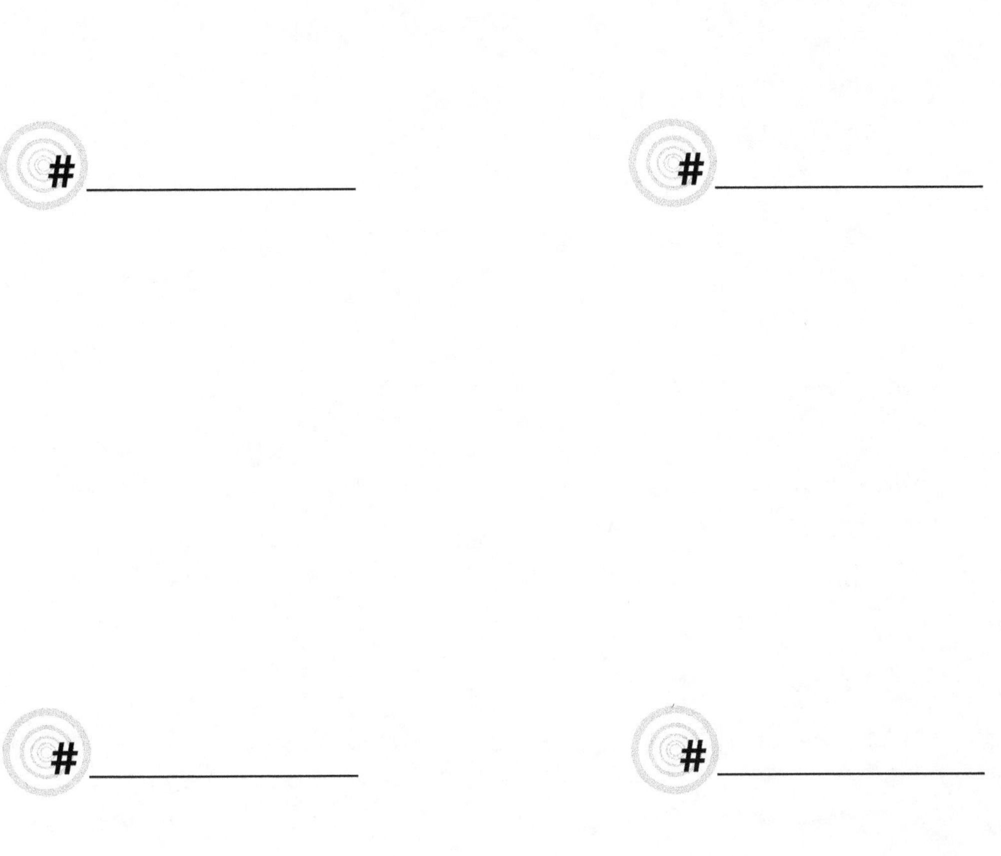

CRITICAL CREATIVITY CROSS-REFERENCE

Use the chart on the following pages for a quick reference to content-area applications in the catalog.

	Math	Science	Social Studies	English Language Arts	Health/ Phycial Education	World Lanugage	Visual & Preforming Arts
Potent Quotables		✓	✓	✓		✓	✓
Résumé Rationale	✓	✓	✓				
Line and Caret			✓	✓	✓	✓	✓
Style Hack		✓	✓	✓	✓		✓
Phrankenword	✓	✓	✓	✓		✓	
Blackout Poetry		✓	✓	✓	✓	✓	
Found Typoetry				✓		✓	✓
Color Palette	✓	✓	✓	✓			
Two Images One Question	✓	✓				✓	

Minimalist Poster	✓		✓	✓			
Mondrian-Ify			✓	✓			✓
Imaged		✓	✓	✓		✓	✓
Emoji Story		✓	✓	✓			✓
Haikonography		✓	✓	✓	✓		
Parody Lyrics		✓	✓	✓			
Audio Landscape		✓	✓	✓			✓
Q-Lisions	✓		✓			✓	✓
Playlist A Life		✓	✓	✓			✓
Score the News	✓	✓	✓			✓	✓

intention

Song Catching	✓		✓	✓			✓
Soundtracking the Moment				✓	✓	✓	✓
Humojis	✓	✓	✓		✓		
Custom Signage		✓		✓	✓		
Dallowinian Party		✓	✓	✓		✓	
Machine Made		✓	✓	✓	✓		
Sensory Map		✓	✓	✓			✓
Tableau Repreaux		✓	✓	✓	✓		
Chronological Choreography		✓		✓		✓	✓
Oreo Challenge		✓	✓	✓	✓		

Board Game Remix		✓	✓	✓	✓		
Book Stack Summary	✓	✓	✓	✓	✓		✓
Metaphorical Architecture			✓	✓			
Five Course Meal		✓		✓		✓	
Metaphorical Fashion		✓	✓				✓
Brick-a-Book	✓	✓				✓	
Hashmash			✓	✓	✓		
One Word to Rule Them All					✓	✓	✓
Character Gallery			✓	✓	✓		
Gif Story		✓	✓	✓			

Volley							
Fauxial Media Profiles							
Belief Board							

HOW TO CRUSH IT WITH CREATIVITY

Find the Wow in the Now

The essence of being human is having a sense of wonder, beauty and poignancy, persistent curiosity, creative thinking, self-awareness, compassion, and empathy. As work becomes more automated, our edge is to work in more human ways; we must, therefore, cultivate these traits. Never stop listening. See rather than merely look. Seek out the ***wabi-sabi*** and the whimsical.

Be Quizzical and Questioning

Nothing innovative ever came from passive acquiescence. Critical consumption means challenging assumptions, exploring perspectives, and not taking things at face value. Hold ideas askew.

Value the Visceral

Go with your gut. Intuition and wonder are essential in the creative process. Take time to linger in the question, experience "wonderlust" about unanswerable topics, and seek opportunities to interact with the environment around you. Intuition should be respected—even in math and science—as a powerful force.

Make Disciplines Dance Together

Think thematically. De-silo school subjects. Reflect about how your learning is connected. Interdisciplinary units of inquiry result in relevance.

Feed Your Meraki

Meraki is a Greek term for putting your love and soul into something creative. As humans, we value what we make ourselves. We want our work to touch people—to make them think or move them in some way. Aim for poignancy—to "prick" another's mind or emotions.

Master the Metaphor

Thinking in analogies and metaphors helps you make the connections that are at the heart of creativity, as well as communicate complex ideas, thus amplifying them.

Clock Your Creativity

We need a daily diet of creativity. Creativity can come in waves, but it can also be scheduled. It need not be a grandiose project—it can bubble forth in a daily endeavor set as a routine. Over time, these efforts accumulate into something more significant or result in a sharpening of skills.

Incubate to Innovate

Creativity needs white space. Incubation means stepping away from the creative endeavor and chilling out, reflecting, or doing something mundane. The best ideas come when walking, swimming, showering, etc., but it's crucial to have a place to pin them down. Think of ideas as butterflies and the notebook as a net.

Miss Your Mark So You Can Find Your Target

Just make it. Second-guessing serves no one. Waiting for the muse is futile. As Picasso said: "Inspiration exists but it has to find you working." Tinker with tools; play with possibilities. You can fail and iterate, as long as you can overcome the inner critic and perils of perfectionism.

Think beyond Your Schtick

The ability to reinvent yourself, to "kill your darlings" if needed, and to diversify and not adhere to one particular medium or style is at the crux of creativity.

SUPPLY CLOSET

Websites

bit.ly/makedujour
(Amy's creativity community)

Brainpickings.org

BriefBox

Colourlovers.com

Five-Card Flickr

Giphy.com

HitRECord

Pecha Flickr

PicMonkey

Projeqt

storify.com

Soundcloud

thenounproject.com

Weebly

Wix

Apps

Clips (iOS)

Enlight

Flipgrid

G Suite for Education

GarageBand

ImgPlay

iMovie

Instagram

Keynote

LinkedIn

MegaPhoto

MojiMaker

Over

Padlet

Pages

Paper by Fifty-Three (iOS)

Pinterest

Post-It Plus (iOS)

Snapchat

Splice by GoPro

StopMotion Studio Pro

Thinglink

TodaysMeet

Twitter

WordFoto

YouTube

Analog

- Action figures
- Colored pencils
- Crayons
- Dice
- Dry erase markers
- Duct tape
- Earbuds
- External microphone
- Glass beads/pebbles
- Glue sticks
- Golf balls
- Graph paper
- Hot glue guns
- Industrial strength Velcro (great for hanging a tablet to the wall)
- Jenga blocks
- LEGO bricks
- Manilla folders
- Marbles
- Masking tape
- Old magazines
- Old newspapers
- Oreo cookies
- Painter's tape
- Paper clips
- Play-Doh
- Rubber bands
- Rulers and tape measures
- Scissors
- Scotch tape
- Scrap wood
- Sharpies of all sizes
- Sticky notes
- Yarn/string
- **Yes And . . . ?**

SOME OF THE MANY BOOKS WE LOVE

The Augmented Mind, Derrick de Kerckhove

Big Magic, Elizabeth Gilbert

Creative Confidence, Tom and David Kelley

The Doodle Revolution, Sunni Brown

Drive, Daniel Pink

How Music Works, David Byrne

The Medium Is the Massage, Marshall McLuhan

Mrs. Dalloway, Virginia Woolf

The Nerdist Way, Chris Hardwick

NetSmart: How to Thrive Online, Howard Rheingold

On Writing, Stephen King

Show Your Work, Austin Kleon

Smarter Than You Think, Clive Thompson

Steal Like an Artist, Austin Kleon

Steal Like an Artist: The Journal, Austin Kleon

The Sketchnote Handbook, Mike Rohde

Think Like an Artist...And Lead a More Creative, Productive Life, Will Gompertz

Understanding Comics, Scott McCloud

Unflattening, Nick Sousanis

Watchmen, Alan Moore and Dave Gibbons

Where Good Ideas Come From, Steven Johnson

A Whole New Mind, Daniel Pink

You're a Genius All the Time, Jack Kerouac

#Hashknowledgments

#StudentCenteredSynergy

#YouthBrigadesOfThe207AndThe808

#FederationOfFamilyAndFriends

#ContinuingCollegialCollaboratorium

#WillingAndDainMegAndBlake

#ChampionsOfWhimsy

#IlluminatiOfWhatIfAndWhyNot

#ThoseThatRemindUsTheHoursAreOurs

#EdupunksAndBoomshakalakas

#KeysAndAnchorsInHallwaysAndHallwaysForAlways

#CreativeSoulmatesWithWhatsAppWisdom

#ThoseWhoEmbraceOurScarsAndFoiblesAndKookiness

#NachosWithBigSaladKennyRogersChickenAndDrinkingTheFat

#SerendipitousSXSWTexMex

#TwitterverseAndTheGooglePlex

#FindYourTribe

#GrowTheTribe

Bibliography

Cleese, John. "Lecture on Creativity." Lecture, ***Video Arts,*** n.p., 1991.

Dumas, Denis and Kevin N. Dunbar. "The Creative Stereotype Effect." PLoS One 11(2):e0142534. doi.org/10.1371/journal.pone.0142567.

Godin, Seth. ***Linchpin: Are You Indispensable?*** New York: Portfolio, 2010.

Jarmush, Jim. "Jim Jarmush's Golden Rules." ***MovieMaker Magazine*** 53 (Winter 2004).

Jenkins, Henry. ***Confronting the Challenges of Participatory Culture: Media Education for the 21st Century.*** Chicago: The MacArthur Foundation. Accessed April 30, 2017. wheatoncollege.edu/president/files/2012/03/Confronting-Challenges-of-Participatory-Culture.pdf.

Kleon, Austin. ***Show Your Work!: 10 Ways to Show Your Creativity and Get Discovered.*** New York: Workman Publishing Co., 2014.

Lessing, Doris. ***The Four-Gated City***, 1969. Reprint, New York: Harper Collins, 2012.

McLuhan, Marshall. ***The Meaning Is the Massage: An Inventory of Effects.*** N.p.: Bantam Books, 1967.

Norton, Michael I., Daniel Mochon, and Dan Ariely. ***The "IKEA Effect": When Labor Leads to Love.*** Cambridge, MA: Harvard Business School, 2011. Accessed April 30, 2017. hbs.edu/faculty/Publication%20Files/11-091.pdf.

More Books from EdTechTeam Press

edtechteam.com/books

The HyperDoc Handbook

Digital Lesson Design Using Google Apps

By Lisa Highfill, Kelly Hilton, and Sarah Landis

The HyperDoc Handbook is a practical reference guide for all K–12 educators who want to transform their teaching into blended-learning environments. ***The HyperDoc Handbook*** is a bestselling book that strikes the perfect balance between pedagogy and how-to tips while also providing ready-to-use lesson plans to get you started with HyperDocs right away.

Innovate with iPad

Lessons to Transform Learning

By Karen Lirenman and Kristen Wideen

Written by two primary teachers, this book provides a complete selection of clearly explained, engaging, open-ended lessons to change the way you use iPads with students at home or in the classroom. It features downloadable task cards, student-created examples, and extension ideas to use with your students. Whether you have access to one iPad for your entire class or one for each student, these lessons will help you transform learning in your classroom.

Assessment That Matters

Using Technology to Personalize Learning

By Kim Meldrum

In ***Assessment That Matters,*** Kim Meldrum explains the three types of assessments—assessment **as** learning, assessment **for** learning, and assessment **of** learning. Within her instruction on gathering rich assessment information, you'll find simple strategies and tips for using today's technology to allow students to demonstrate learning in creative and innovative ways.

Classroom Management in the Digital Age

Effective Practices for Technology-Rich Learning Spaces

By Patrick Green and Heather Dowd

Classroom Management in the Digital Age helps guide and support teachers through the new landscape of device-rich classrooms. It provides practical strategies to novice and expert educators alike who want to maximize learning and minimize distraction. Learn how to keep up with the times while limiting time-wasters and senseless screen-staring time.

The Space

A Guide for Educators

By Rebecca Louise Hare and Robert Dillon

The Space supports the conversation around revolution happening in education today concerning the reshaping of school spaces. This book goes well beyond the ideas for learning-space design that focuses on Pinterest-perfect classrooms and instead discusses real and practical ways to design learning spaces that support and drive learning.

A Learner's Paradise

How New Zealand Is Reimagining Education

By Richard Wells

What if teachers were truly trusted to run education? In ***A Learner's Paradise,*** Richard Wells outlines New Zealand's forward-thinking education system in which teachers are empowered to do exactly that. With no prescribed curriculum, teachers and students work together to create individualized learning plans—all the way through the high-school level. From this guidebook, you'll learn how New Zealand is reimagining education and setting an example for innovative educators, parents, and school districts to follow.

The Google Apps Guidebook

Lessons, Activities, and Projects Created by Students for Teachers

By Kern Kelley and the Tech Sherpas

The Google Apps Guidebook is filled with great ideas for the classroom from the voice of the students themselves. Each chapter introduces an engaging project that teaches students (and teachers) how to use one of Google's powerful tools. Projects are differentiated for a variety of age ranges and can be adapted for most content areas.

Dive into Inquiry

Amplify Learning and Empower Student Voice

By Trevor MacKenzie

Dive into Inquiry beautifully marries the voice and choice of inquiry with the structure and support required to optimize learning. With ***Dive into Inquiry***, you'll gain an understanding of how to best support your learners as they shift from a traditional learning model into the inquiry classroom where student agency is fostered and celebrated each and every day.

Sketchnotes for Educators

100 Inspiring Illustrations for Lifelong Learners

By Sylvia Duckworth

Sketchnotes for Educators contains 100 of Sylvia Duckworth's most popular sketchnotes, with links to the original downloads that can be used in class or shared with colleagues. Interspersed throughout the book are reflections from Sylvia about what motivated her to create the drawings as well as commentary from many of the educators whose work inspired her sketchnotes.

Code in Every Class

How All Educators Can Teach Programming

By Kevin Brookhouser and Ria Megnin

In ***Code in Every Class***, Kevin Brookhouser and Ria Megnin explain why computer science is critical to your students' future success. With lesson ideas and step-by-step instruction, they show you how to take tech education into your own hands and open a world of opportunities to your students. And here's the best news: You ***don't*** have to be a computer genius to teach the basics of coding.

Making Your School Something Special

Enhance Learning, Build Confidence, and Foster Success at Every Level

By Rushton Hurley

In ***Making Your School Something Special***, educator and international speaker Rushton Hurley explores the mindsets, activities, and technology that make for great learning. You'll learn how to create strong learning activities and make your school a place where students and teachers alike want to be—because it's where they feel energized, inspired, and ***special***.

The Google Infused Classroom

Transformative Lessons You Can Use in Your Classroom Tomorrow

By Holly Clark and Tanya Avrith

This beautifully designed book offers step-by-step guidance on using technology to design instruction that allows students to show their thinking, demonstrate their learning, and share their work (and voices!) with authentic audiences. ***The Google Infused Classroom*** will equip you to empower your students to use technology in meaningful ways that prepare them for the future.

The Google Cardboard Book

Explore, Engage, and Educate with Virtual Reality

An EdTechTeam Collaboration

In ***The Google Cardboard Book***, EdTechTeam trainers and leaders offer step-by-step instructions on how to use virtual reality technology in your classroom—no matter what subject you teach. You'll learn what tools you need (and how affordable they can be), which apps to start with, and how to view, capture, and share 360° videos and images.

Transforming Libraries

A Toolkit for Innovators, Makers, and Seekers

By Ron Starker

In the Digital Age, it's more important than ever for libraries to evolve into gathering points for collaboration, spaces for innovation, and places where authentic learning occurs. In ***Transforming Libraries***, Ron Starker reveals ways to make libraries makerspaces, innovation centers, community commons, and learning design studios that engage multiple forms of intelligence.

Sign up to learn more about new and upcoming books at **bit.ly/edtechteambooks**

BRING MORE INTENTION & RIGOROUS WHIMSY TO YOUR PROFESSIONAL DEVELOPMENT

Dan and Amy offer a number of keynote presentations and workshop experiences, including one that focuses on the message and activities in ***Intention***. They also offer online courses in critical creativity, meaningful making, and uncovering intention.

Some of Amy's most popular offerings include . . .

Image Is Everything: Exploring Critical Thinking with Visual Literacies

From cave walls to Facebook walls, we have always embraced visual communication. With the changing media landscape, our streams, memes, and zines have exploded with imagery, ushering in a need for visual literacy skills. We are quickly moving from images as decoration and augmentation to images as sole content and communication tools. Images can essentialize the cumbersome in beautiful ways. They have a "stickiness" for the viewer and challenge the critical thinking of the creator.

This hands-on session explores the "whys" of visual literacy and offers participants an opportunity to tinker and play with iconography and metaphorical thinking, emojis, GIFs, memes, graphic design, infographics, sketchnotes, photography, and video.

Participants experiment with ways to use visual language for personal knowledge management, amplification of knowledge and creative work, critical thinking, social interaction (conversation), and other forms of creative and intellectual expression.

RemixED: The Power of Remix, Mashup, and Re-contextualization in the Classroom

Our students are engrossed in remix culture—they are the appropriation and re-contextualization generation. Remix calls for knowledge and understanding, critical, higher-order, and design thinking, a variety of tech skills, and, frequently, collaboration and navigation in the greater media landscape. Most importantly, a remix task offers students a chance to truly transform a work and create something unique—something that will contribute to their digital presence and legacy. This session is part pedagogical/philosophical and part participatory. Attendees will leave with a "goodie bag" of resources and ideas, as well as have the opportunity to develop, practice, and share several types of remix projects.

Get a glimpse into the history of remix in the art world and its significance in our present media landscape. Explore how different techniques of remix and mashup lend themselves to collaborative creativity and differentiation in the classroom. Look into the distinctions between "remix" and "rip-off" and discuss the ways to help work become transformative rather than mere copies. Find out how social media in particular inspires re-contextualization and reimagining. And, in an era of ever-abbreviated communication, we'll practice various ways to "essentialize" and synthesize into more minimalist, visual interpretations.

What Would da Vinci Do?: Lessons from Great Artists' Lives and Creative Processes

While an artist's **oeuvres** might be the thing that garners the most attention, what drives them and makes them tick is often the most intriguing. We can gain valuable insight by peering into artists' lives and creative processes and applying what we learn to our own intellectual and creative pursuits. What big takeaways from the likes of da Vinci, Michelangelo, Picasso, Van Gogh, and others can help us rethink our teaching, working, and living?

This session/talk is for anyone interested in how creativity works and how to foster creative thinking, perseverance, and resilience in oneself and one's students.

(This presentation can be given as a keynote format, varying in length from ten to sixty minutes, but can also be crafted into a hands-on participatory session)

Mobile Sapiens: Found Art and Story Scavenger-Hunt Safari

In this scavenger-hunt-style safari, participants need a sense of adventure, a mobile phone (list of relevant apps will be shared before the event), and a desire to create some found art and narrative as they interact with their surrounding environment. Experimenting with found art sharpens one's senses and better prepares the mind for creative thinking—that is, connecting dots in unique ways. Attendees can participate individually or on a team as they explore, create, and share with the rest of the group. Get ready to hone your playfulness and creativity and learn some engaging activities to try with students. You will leave this workshop seeing the world in a different way.

Some of Dan's most popular offerings include . . .

Literary Remix: Uncovering Meaning in the ELA Classroom Through Mashing up and Reinvention

Explore the impact of remixes and mashups on the world of literary analysis. Poetry, prose, drama: No literary form is too sacred to be reinvented in the name of better understanding. Learn how strategies such as Literary 3x3 and Rose/Bud/Thorn open doorways, and how a balance of analog and digital tools can turn students into more active analysts and creators.

Potent Quotables: Transforming Text into Powerful Visuals

When students fuse meaningful text with engaging imagery, they create products that demonstrate deeper understanding and prove greater than the sum of their parts. Learn how students might apply graphic-design principles and royalty-free images to digital tools to make social-media-worthy visuals. Also discover feedback and critique protocols students may use throughout your classroom.

The Improviser's Mindset: Improv in the Classroom and Beyond

There will be games, shenanigans, and tools to bring back to the classroom. And there will be an exploration of how the principles of acceptance, communication, and trust can transform our approach toward problem solving and understanding. Participants can expect the opportunity to develop a playlist of improv games and exercises to apply in their impact areas.

To Solve a Mockingbird: Design Thinking the Content

How might we develop more authentic literacy skills through the process of human-centered, empathy-fueled problem solving? Learn the essentials of design thinking, discover ways in which those principles may be applied to the classroom, and start developing a learning experience to bring to your students.

Dan and Amy also design customized sessions to meet your needs, whether at the team, building, district, or organizational level.

Learn more at edtechteam.com/books.

For more information, contact press@edtechteam.com.

#CriticalCreativity @IntentionBook

#IntentionTheBook IntentionTheBook.Online